REDESIGNING THE AEROPLANE
WHILE FLYING

REDESIGNING THE AEROPLANE WHILE FLYING

Reforming Institutions

Arun Maira

RAINLIGHT
RUPA

Published in Rainlight by
Rupa Publications India Pvt. Ltd 2014
7/16, Ansari Road, Daryaganj
New Delhi 110002

Sales centres:
Allahabad Bengaluru Chennai
Hyderabad Jaipur Kathmandu
Kolkata Mumbai

Copyright © Arun Maira 2014

All rights reserved.
No part of this publication may be reproduced, transmitted,
or stored in a retrieval system, in any form or by any means, electronic,
mechanical, photocopying, recording or otherwise, without the prior
permission of the publisher.

ISBN: 978-81-291-3126-3

First impression 2014

10 9 8 7 6 5 4 3 2 1

The moral right of the author has been asserted.

Printed at Replika Press Pvt. Ltd., India

This book is sold subject to the condition that it shall not, by way
of trade or otherwise, be lent, resold, hired out, or otherwise circulated,
without the publisher's prior consent, in any form of binding or cover
other than that in which it is published.

CONTENTS

Preface	*vii*
Introduction	*xiii*
The Storm and the Earthquake	1
India in Transition	12
The Rules of the Game	39
Redesigning the Aeroplane While Flying	59
Monitoring and Controlling	83
Redefining Success: New Scorecards	102
Democracy and Divisions	126
Consensus and Trust	145
How on Earth Can We Live Together	160
Visions of the Future	184
Acknowledgements	*197*
References	*202*

PREFACE

I have been writing this book for almost twenty years, though it came together only in the last four.

Twenty years ago it became very clear that the principal question I was pursuing in my work was: 'How can people work more effectively together to produce the outcomes they want?' I was then with Arthur D. Little Inc. (ADL) in Cambridge, Massachusetts, the oldest consulting company in the world, consulting for business organizations in the USA, Mexico and India. We consulted with NASA and the US government too.

My colleagues in ADL assisted their clients with advice on technology strategy, product and market strategies, and operations management. Many of ADL's clients were demanding that the consultants do not leave a report of what should be done. They must ensure that their recommendations are implemented too. Implementation invariably required that the leadership of the client organization and the people within it do many different things than what they were doing and/or do the same things, but differently. This would require changes in behaviour and changes in mindsets—'changing our culture', as many clients put it. Changing cultures, mindsets and behaviours—the 'how' of change—is the hardest part, they would say. Describing 'what' must be done is much easier.

The consultants wanted new toolkits to assist their clients to make the culture changes necessary. The consultants had to change their own mindsets too, to work alongside their clients and coach them through the process of implementation, rather than prescribe solutions to them. My colleagues in ADL turned to me. After some successful client engagements, they urged me to write a book codifying the practice of making change happen. So I wrote my first book, *The Accelerating Organization: Embracing the Human Face of Change,* along with a colleague, Dr Peter Scott-Morgan, which was published by McGraw Hill in the USA in 1996.

On my return to India in 2000, I was asked to assist many partnerships to perform: partnerships between business organizations; partnerships between government and business organizations; and partnerships between civil society, government and business organizations. Getting people within a client organization, whether business or government, to work together to produce the results they want, is easy as compared to getting people to collaborate across organizational boundaries. In a single organization people are under one command. It is set up for a clear purpose. It has its own rules, written as well as unwritten, that guide its members' behaviour. When two or more organizations must work together to create results for a larger system, collaboration amongst their members is much more difficult to obtain. Who is the boss in these initiatives? Which organization's rules will be adopted? Whose culture will prevail?

Authority within an organization can be used to make the structural changes (reporting relationships, incentive systems, etc.) that can induce the changes of behaviour required to implement the new strategy. But when many organizations must work together, it is difficult to change the behaviour of partners who belong to different organizations with such structural changes. Then other means must be found to create the alignment towards the goal, and bring about the necessary cooperation to produce the required results. A deeply shared aspiration for an outcome that all want is one of the means, and agreement about the rules of conduct that all partners will voluntarily adopt is another. My work with partnerships and inquiries into the structures they require for high performance resulted in my next book, *Shaping the Future: Aspirational Leadership in India and Beyond,* published by John Wiley and Sons in 2002.

Many of the challenges that humanity must address now, such as the degradation of the environment and climate change, persistent inequities within and across countries, and fair rules for global trade, require collaboration across national boundaries. Difficulties in effecting democratic agreements for the improvement of the global commons amongst national governments, each of whom is accountable to its own citizens, have been stalling progress. Methods for arriving at voluntary arrangements are required, in which the mighty and the majority do not smother the weak and the minority.

Indian democracy is founded on a good constitution. India conducts fair and efficient elections on a scale no other country does. Yet the evolution of Indian democracy requires efficient processes for deliberation amongst citizens for the country to move together and faster to produce the outcomes all want. Fully democratic societies require both: constitutions that guarantee rights and due process as well as good, institutionalized processes for conduct of deliberations amongst their members. I was called upon many times, in India and elsewhere, to design and conduct deliberations amongst divergent stakeholders on a variety of issues. I researched the methods used in many countries and described processes for obtaining consensus in my book, *Discordant Democrats: Five Steps to Consensus,* published by Penguin in 2007.

Two years later, in July 2009, I was unexpectedly invited by the prime minister of India, Dr Manmohan Singh, to serve as a member of the country's Planning Commission. When the Planning Commission was set up in 1950, the aspiration was to create an institution that would make plans with the people for the people. According to its numerous critics, it has become an ivory tower disconnected from realities on the ground with a bureaucracy that is ineffectual in inducing change in the country. One of the tasks the PM gave me on the side, in addition to my official responsibilities, was to consider how the Planning Commission could be reformed to become a 'system reforms commission' and 'an essay in persuasion' as it should be, rather than the budget-allocating, plan-formulating and target-setting organization it has become.

For the past four years, from India's cockpit—the national Planning Commission—I could get a perspective of the changes sweeping through India. Every year, chief ministers of all Indian states come to the Planning Commission to explain the progress their states are making and the challenges they are facing. The Planning Commission oversees the central government ministries too, and all sectors of the Indian economy. When it prepared the country's 12th Five Year Plan in 2012, it deployed a process for the first time to listen widely to the people of the country. Almost a thousand civil society organizations representing all sections of Indian society and dozens of business associations participated in an exercise to gather the views of citizens about what mattered most to them and the opportunities they saw for change in the country. With these myriad inputs from many perspectives, and using techniques of systems analysis and scenario planning, one could see the principal forces that are shaping India. And one could hear the signals beneath the deep rumbling of Indian democracy.

In these four years I have looked into India's progress through the lens of 'system reforms' as the prime minister asked me to, and I have also struggled mightily to change the ways in which the Planning Commission itself functions. Facing these challenges, I re-examined my insights into the ways of reforming institutions that I had found and written about over the previous fifteen years. And I searched further.

Many countries, including India, are looking for better ways, for more sustainable and more inclusive development of societies. In the last ten years, there has been virulent criticism of the roles that financial institutions and regulators have played in the global economic crisis. The responsibilities of the state vis-à-vis private enterprises for ensuring employment for youth, for providing accessible, affordable, and acceptable quality healthcare, and for providing other public goods equitably, have also been questioned. At the same time, shortcomings of the disciplines of economics, especially macro-economics, have become evident to policy-makers. From my vantage in the Indian Planning Commission, I was able to connect with many organizations and many remarkable persons in India and other countries who are inquiring into multi-faceted issues of institutional reform.

Institutions provide order to our lives. When institutions in their present forms cannot provide us the satisfactions we want, they must be reformed. However, when these institutions begin to change, we fear the loss of stability their existing order has provided. So we resist the change, even though we want change. I compare this insecurity with the risks taken when redesigning an aeroplane while flying in it.

In *Redesigning the Aeroplane While Flying: Reforming Institutions*, I have put together several inter-related concepts about the multi-faceted and complex process of reforming institutions that I have learned in the past twenty years. Thus is not an academic book, though I have read quite extensively on the subject. Rather, it combines preaching with practice, and some walking with talking.

In the end, this book is not a prescription of the specific institutional reforms India needs, or the specific reforms that any other country needs. Institutions must fit their contexts. They must be changed with active engagement of their stakeholders. Prescriptions of which institutions should be changed and what their designs should be would be like consultants' reports of 'what' is required. As explained before, the 'how' of implementing the reforms is always the greater challenge. Therefore I have focused my book on the process of redesigning the aeroplane while flying, rather than what the design of the aeroplane should be.

INTRODUCTION

The hope of the world is the man who keeps right on, changing his methods if he must, but not his purpose.

—HERBERT CASSON

John F. Kennedy's call in 1961 to America to put a man on the moon stirred the world's imagination. The objective, which seemed way beyond reach when he announced it, was reached within a decade. It was made possible with the development of vehicles that could operate in the rarefied atmosphere of space. When Kennedy made his speech, jet planes were flying across oceans. Aeronautical technology had come a long way since the design of the plane the Wright brothers had flown for just 300 yards to the amazement of the world in 1903. But the conditions in space are very different to those in the earth's atmosphere. Therefore, the mission to the moon required the development of radically new vehicles that could operate in those conditions.

Institutions—of the state, of business, of democracy, of justice—have been developed by human beings, over centuries, to fulfil the needs of their societies. Institutions are the vehicles with which societies realize their aspirations. Indeed, the species of Homo sapiens can be distinguished from other animal species by its *deliberate* development of institutions for the management of its affairs. Animal, bird and insect communities have innate, institutionalized rules that govern their behaviour. But so far as we know they do not, unlike human beings, consciously change and improve these institutionalized rules.

Four forces that had been gaining strength for some time have collided in the last ten years. They are: capitalism and free markets as the way to organize economies; democracy and the principles of human rights as the way to organize societies; the growing awareness of the limits of the earth to support human economic enterprise as presently designed; and an explosion in the availability of information to people everywhere through technologies of communication and digitization. The combination of these forces has dramatically changed the conditions in which institutions of democracy, government, capitalism, and business must operate. Just as aircraft designed for atmospheric flight cannot operate safely—or at all—in open space, we now need a fundamental redesign of many institutions.

The mismatch between the design of institutions and the conditions in which they must perform can be gauged by the increasing mistrust of citizens in the institutions that govern their lives. The World Economic Forum (WEF) unveiled a major global public opinion survey in 2002. The 'Voice of the People' survey of 36,000 people in forty-seven countries disclosed a dramatic lack of trust in democratic institutions (i.e. parliament, congress, etc.). Two thirds of those surveyed said they disagreed that their country is 'governed by the will of the people'. The survey found that global companies and large domestic companies were equally distrusted to operate in the best interest of society, ranking them next to national legislative bodies at the bottom of the trust ratings. José Maria Figueres, managing director of the WEF, said: 'Our institutions are under tremendous pressure to evolve. It is clear that collective action is needed to rebuild the bridge of trust between citizens and their institutions.'

In the ten years since then the global economy has been roiled by the financial crisis that rolled out from the United States (US).

Citizens were dismayed that the US government, and governments in other Western countries too, had not regulated big financial institutions sufficiently, resulting in hardships for millions of people who lost their homes, their savings and their jobs. People were very angry that leaders of financial institutions had personally accumulated millions of dollars of wealth while the masses were suffering. Clearly, the WEF's warning to fix institutions had not been heeded. The 2013 Edelman Trust Barometer, an annual survey of citizens' trust in institutions, revealed how low trust had sunk. Only18 per cent said they trusted business leaders to tell the truth, and even less, 13 per cent, trusted government leaders. Only 19 per cent trusted business leaders and 14 per cent trusted government leaders to make ethical and moral decisions.

The reform of institutions has become imperative. How shall it be done? The danger of summarizing my argument in advance is oversimplification. Yet I want to give you a sense of it.

Reforming institutions is not easy. If institutions are the vehicles in which we are travelling, then we must 'redesign the aircraft while we are flying it'. This is a difficult, even dangerous, exercise and so there is resistance to institutional reform.

'Institutions' are not merely 'organizations' with their hierarchies and budgets, though they are often thought of as only that. Institutions are also the processes by which societies perform functions. Institutions also include the norms by which societies conduct themselves. Therefore, institutional reform cannot be achieved only by redrawing organization charts or creating new organizations with old templates. Implicit 'theories-in-use', at the back of our heads, that have guided us so far have to be made transparent and changed. This can be very discomforting. Yet this is the deep level at which institutional reforms have to be made as we fly into the new millennium. We cannot merely redesign the seats in the aeroplane when it must fly out of the atmosphere into space. We have to change its structure more fundamentally.

Man's desire to be in charge of the world, and even to reorder the world to suit man, mentally places him outside the system that he wishes to redesign and control. In reality man is only a component of the world and is embedded within it.

Thus we have two different models of systems. The first is an engineer sitting outside his machine tinkering with it. The second is an organic system with every agent within it dependent on others, none able to isolate itself from the systems' reactions to its own actions. Related to these two models of systems are two fundamental laws of science. The first is the Second Law of Thermodynamics that every engineer must learn. It says that the entropy (or useless energy) of a complex system must increase with time. Therefore, the capability of any complex machine will reduce with time. The other law—of evolutionary biology—says that the capabilities of complex systems will evolve and increase with time!

These two laws that we see in operation all around us seem contradictory. I will explain their difference and also reconcile them. Clues to how to redesign an aircraft while flying in it, which is the challenge in reforming institutions, emerge from this analysis.

Scientific disciplines and engineering methods have undoubtedly helped man to improve the world for himself. Science and engineering are founded on requirements for objectivity and measurement. The pursuit of numbers, in the belief that numbers alone indicate accuracy, has become the bane of economics. Many forces that shape societies and economies cannot be easily measured such as the trust of citizens in institutions. Such substantial forces must not be excluded from a model which seeks to explain the behaviour of the economy. Many economists insist on equations and numbers because that is all their computers can process, whereas economists should study human behaviour as it is, not as they find easy to model.

Alan Greenspan, former chairman of the US Federal Reserve, wrote the mea culpa for the global economic crisis, on behalf of all economists, in *Foreign Affairs* (Greenspan 2013):

> What went wrong? Why was virtually every economist and policy-maker of note so blind to the coming calamity? How did so many experts, including me, fail to see it approaching? I have come to see that an important part of the answers to those questions is a very old idea: "animal spirits", the term Keynes famously coined in 1936.... Keynes was hardly the first person to note the importance of irrational factors in economic decision-making, and economists surely did not lose sight of their significance in the decades that followed. The trouble is that such behavior is hard to measure and stubbornly resistant to any systematic analysis. For decades, most economists, including me, had concluded that irrational factors could not fit into any reliable method of forecasting.

Too much of reality has been left out of mainstream economists' models for them to explain the world. These flawed models are incapable of predicting the future condition of an economy. The reconstruction of economics will require the inclusion of many disciplines of social and ecological sciences in a collaborative inquiry. Human societies and economies are complex systems. To see the whole elephant, those who have blinded themselves to others' points of view by their conceptual and ideological differences must come together. I will explain concepts of systems thinking and scenario planning that can enable people to pool their perspectives to see the whole elephant.

Scenario planning was applied three times in India since 2000 to understand the forces shaping the country and to locate the leverage points for change and policy action. In 2000, a large, diverse group of Indians carried out an exercise outside the official system to experiment with the techniques and see what they could not see with conventional tools of economics and policy analysis. In 2005, using these insights, the WEF conducted a more rigorous exercise in collaboration with the Confederation of Indian Industry (CII). The scenarios prepared in 2005 revealed that the economy, which was accelerating towards 9 per cent growth, would stumble towards 6 per cent in a few years unless institutions were fixed. The warning was not heeded.

In 2011, scenario planning was used 'semi-officially' by India's Planning Commission for the first time, to supplement the preparation of the country's 12th Five Year Plan.

The Planning Commission's scenarios revealed how deep the mistrust of the country's institutions had become. The impact of this mistrust on processes of policymaking and implementation was explained in a system diagram. This rough model of the system, which included forces such as trust and speed of policymaking and implementation, was then used by the National Council of Applied Economic Research (NCAER) to forecast what the growth rates of the Indian economy would be, depending on the pace at which institutions would be reformed. NCAER forecasted that growth of gross domestic product (GDP) would fall below 5 per cent if effective action was not taken immediately. And growth did fall below 5 per cent in 2013 much to the consternation of the country's official economic managers and advisers. They had been hoping against hope that their much higher forecasts would come true. They could not because their forecasts were not founded on a complete model.

Managers and economists are wont to say, 'You can only manage what you can measure.' Measurement systems can become blinkers, shutting out what they cannot measure. Our vision of the world must be broadened from what we know how to measure to all that is important, even if we do not know how to measure all of it yet. I will discuss the emergence of new 'balanced' scorecards that extend beyond economic measures such as GDP and per capita incomes of countries, and revenues and profits of business enterprises, to include assessments of the health of the environment and communities.

An institution's scorecard, be it a government or a business corporation, must express the institution's contract with its stakeholders. It must enable the managers of the institution to measure how well they are doing in delivering what is expected of them. The scorecard is also a means of accounting to the institution's stakeholders.

Redesigning institutions is a complex process. Members of organizations and societies must allow their institutions to change. In fact, the behaviours of their members are an essential ingredient of institutions. Therefore, the involvement of people is necessary for any significant institutional reform. Let us revert to our metaphor of redesigning the aeroplane while flying in it. So long as the aeroplane is cruising on autopilot, the passengers can lie back undisturbed. Whenever the pilot encounters turbulent conditions or must carry out emergency procedures, the passengers must also play their part to ensure their own safety and the safety of others. At these times, the pilot must explain what is happening and what is required of the passengers.

When the support of people is required for change, they must have a vision of what the change will produce for them and why it is necessary. Great leaders bring about change by engaging people with a vision. To prepare their country for the civil rights legislation, President Lyndon B. Johnson gave Americans a vision of 'a great society' that they would be proud of and they would have to shape: a society in which all citizens, black or white, would be equal. Nelson Mandela united a deeply divided South Africa with a vision of a 'rainbow nation'.

While people may agree with the outcomes a vision offers, they can be deeply divided about the means to obtain them. Should government have a larger role or a smaller role? Should there be more GDP growth with fewer taxes for the rich first, or should there be more inclusion with schemes for universal health care and education? Ideological divisions can make agreement about the means, and even the ends, very difficult. I will present some conflicting beliefs about the ways things should be that confound current debates about economic development and human progress. My purpose in presenting these divisions will be not to resolve them. It is to propose the architectures of processes necessary for people to resolve these matters amongst themselves.

Consensual democracies require many institutions and processes for deliberation amongst people. Not only must large numbers of people be engaged, but different constituents must listen to each other too for consensus.

Modern communication technologies seem to provide the means to listen to the masses. Millions can express themselves in tweets and posts on social media platforms. However, as policymakers using these mediums of communication have realized, the vast reach and speed of these mediums may make democratic communication more difficult, not less.

What is the signal that emerges from all that chatter and noise on social media platforms? And, how does one ensure that democratic principles are at work when obtaining inputs electronically? Are some technology-savvy people 'stuffing the ballot boxes' with multiple responses, whereas the views of many not so savvy are not being counted at all?

When there are ideological differences amongst persons and organizations, there is much greater reluctance to meet others who they consider the opposition. This makes deliberation amongst the people much more difficult. Sections of citizens may agree on what 'people like them' want. However, citizens cannot come to an agreement about what 'we, all the people' really want.

The ubiquity of information with which people are being bombarded through the Internet, social media and multiple 24x7 news channels has surpassed human capacities—biological and mental—for the amount of information that a person can process at any one time. Therefore, to cope with the increasing 'attention deficit disorder' that we are suffering from with information overload, we must consciously or unconsciously choose what and who we pay attention to. We must choose the channels and Internet communities we will connect with, and the opinion makers we will follow.

Our choices will be, inevitably, guided by our underlying beliefs about the sort of ideas and people we like and those we do not. Thus people are being driven into 'conceptually gated communities' in which they listen to people with the same beliefs. And they shut out others who may have fundamentally different beliefs.

I will outline a framework for democratic decision making. Consensus is a word much bandied about. Consensus is often necessary in societies, especially in democracies. The framework answers questions such as: how is consensus different from unanimity? When is consensus necessary, and when is a majority vote sufficient? And, how can consensus be reached?

The principles for redesigning institutions presented in this book would apply to institutions of government and business in all countries. Indeed, the research and writings I have relied on, as well as the examples I use, are from many countries. However, a single case study often enables several ideas to become connected for the reader. I have used my country, India, as the principal case study to which many ideas in this book are related.

India's ancient Hindu religion is known to welcome people of all faiths. India is the fountainhead of Buddhism and Jainism—two of the world's oldest religions that preach tolerance. The British ruled India for a hundred years. They introduced the English language to the country and with it they gave millions of Indians a window to most of Western thought.

India is where civilizations of the East and West meet. India embraced political democracy at its birth sixty years ago. Then, twenty years ago, it also veered towards free-market capitalism. The opening of markets and unleashing of capitalism in India has undoubtedly accelerated economic growth and wealth has begun to accumulate. Forbes magazine forecasted a few years ago that before 2020 India will have the most billionaires in the world. But for India to realize the 'demographic dividend' from its children, which economists say will propel India to be the third largest economy in the world within three decades, India will have to take care of *all* its children, including the malnourished and undereducated children (who are half the total) and not just the better off.

The development of institutions that conform to both democratic principles as well as market-capitalist ideas is one of human history's unfinished tasks. Perhaps it has become modern India's destiny to help finish the task. The Indian political landscape is churning. Parties of left, right and centre are manoeuvring for elected space. 'While the West often tries to discuss the world in black and white terms, the Indian mind is able to see the world in many different colors,' says Kishore Mahbubani, dean of the Lee Kuan Yew School of Public Policy, in *The New Asian Hemisphere* (2008: 173).

Humanity is on a quest for better outcomes, and a quest for new ways to obtain those outcomes. Human development is a process of collective learning: discovering new insights about the world of which we are a part, and learning from our own and each others' experiences. This book provides some insights and ideas to stimulate the discovery of solutions by people searching for a better way.

This book also provides new ways to think about institutions and about the process of reforming them. It describes a macro-level architecture for new institutions. It does not provide specific solutions for any country. The solutions must be found and implemented through democratic processes in many nations.

1

THE STORM AND THE EARTHQUAKE

There comes a tide in the affairs of men...

—WILLIAM SHAKESPEARE

We are living, as the Chinese would say, in 'interesting times'. I had thought to live in interesting times was a blessing. For many years I would blithely say to friends, 'May you live in interesting times.' Until, one day, a Chinese friend heard me. He pulled me aside to explain that interesting times meant difficult times! Well, the world seems to be in difficult times now. And I say that these are interesting times because there is a need for fundamentally new ideas.

INSTITUTIONS ARE UNDER STRESS GLOBALLY

The Arab Spring uprisings that erupted in 2010 were rebellions by people against the autocratic governments of their countries. In 2013, hundreds of thousands of people in Turkey and Brazil came out on the streets, both countries with democratically elected governments. Their citizens want even more accountable governments. The governments of southern European countries have also been under stress since 2010, with citizens repeatedly on the streets demanding change.

It is not only government institutions that citizens are unhappy with. They are also disillusioned with business institutions. The global financial crisis drew out citizens' anger against financial institutions. Multinational corporations (MNCs) are now being exposed for cleverly managing to disconnect themselves from the countries where they actually have their operations and earn their revenues, by claiming that they earn their revenues and profits in other countries where they do not have to pay any taxes! They are facing the ire of governments, and public anger too. They are also under fire from non-governmental organizations (NGOs) for the damage many of them cause to the natural environment and to the livelihoods of local communities as they expand their operations in the quest for more profits.

International organizations, such as the World Trade Organization (WTO), are proving to be inadequate to equitably manage global trade regulations. The institutions of the European Union (EU) are also under stress. And many countries are banging on the doors of the United Nations Security Council. They complain that the oligopolistic structure created by the victors of the Second World War is an undemocratic anachronism. And, recently, exacerbated by the United States' cyberspace snooping programme, the monopoly of the Internet Corporation for Assigned Names and Numbers (ICANN), a private body in the United States (US), that governs the Internet, is facing criticism from other countries.

From the streets of Cairo where citizens came out in millions yet again in 2013—this time railing against a democratically elected government, through the protests against financial and business institutions—to the Internet, the theme is the demand for reforming institutions.

In India, too, the mismatch between the capability of the country's institutions and what citizens want has become wide.

The millions who came out, led by Anna Hazare in 2011, against corruption in the country, with their demand to make new laws and create new institutions, and the millions more who took to the streets and to social media channels the next year with their anger against the inability of institutions to provide safety to women, were demanding overdue reforms of institutions of governance.

The response of elected parliamentarians of all political parties in India to the Anna Hazare movement was: 'You have elected us, please leave governance to us.' In fact, many ministers said that citizens who demanded that they must participate in shaping new laws were destroying democracy! The same was said by the prime minister of Turkey about the citizens protesting in Taksim Square in Istanbul.

INDIA NEEDS INSTITUTIONAL REFORM URGENTLY

The goal of India's 12th Five Year Plan that commenced in 2012 is 'Faster, Inclusive, and Sustainable Growth'. The country presently is far from this aspirational goal. The growth of the gross domestic product (GDP) had touched almost 10 per cent per annum in some years of the 11th Five Year Plan. But by 2012, GDP growth had worryingly declined to below 6 per cent. During the high growth years, protests against inequities and environmental degradation had been increasing as fast as GDP growth. Protests are now getting more strident.

Clearly, the country needs a plan to accelerate progress on all three tracks simultaneously—economic growth, social inclusion and environmental sustainability. The histories of other nations, as well as India's own recent experience, have shown that this trinity is not easy to realize.

Indian citizens are becoming disillusioned with political parties and government institutions, and even with big businesses that they see as crony capitalists. Therefore, to make the Indian system move, to get faster growth which must be more equitable and sustainable too, it is no longer enough for the government to announce big ticket economic reforms. For those reforms to be supported and then implemented, citizens must have more confidence in institutions. Therefore, institutional reforms must proceed alongside economic reforms. Indeed, some say that institutional reforms must now precede economic reforms so that the capacity of institutions can catch up with the demands that economic reforms are imposing on them.

THE WHY AND THE HOW OF INSTITUTIONAL REFORM

The world is going through interesting times. And the theme everywhere is the need for better institutions. Why has this global institutional crisis arisen? How can we create the institutions we need now?

Institutions—of the state, of business, of democracy, of justice—have been developed by human beings, over centuries, to fulfil the needs of their societies. Institutions are the vehicles with which societies realize their aspirations. Indeed, Homo sapiens can be distinguished from other animal species by their *deliberate* development of institutions for the management of their affairs. Animal, bird and insect communities have innate, institutionalized rules that govern their behaviour. But so far as we know they do not, unlike human beings, consciously change and improve these institutionalized rules.

Many will recollect Neil Armstrong's immortal words when he stepped onto the moon: 'That's one small step for man, one giant leap for mankind.' Armstrong could take mankind a leap further than it had reached before because new vehicles had been developed to take him into space and land him on the moon.

The conditions in which institutions are operating have changed dramatically in the past two decades. The design of institutions must be changed to suit these new conditions. Just as aircraft designed for atmospheric flight cannot operate safely—or at all—in open space, we now need a fundamental redesign of many institutions. It is no longer enough to change the design of the seats inside the aeroplane: the basic structure of the craft must change. Similarly, it is no longer enough to tinker with institutions, or to merely change personnel at the top. The structures of institutions must be fundamentally changed.

THE MORE THAN PERFECT STORM

The forces shaping our future are having a seismic effect on the institutions of democracy, capitalism and government. I will use two images to visualize these forces and their implications. One is an image of a storm; the other is an image of a globe in stress.

First, let us study the image of the storm. Many of who have read Sebastian Junger's book with the eponymous title will recollect the 'perfect storm' that Junger describes. Not two, but three storm systems converged in the North Atlantic. This was unprecedented. No ship had been designed for such conditions. And no captain had the skills to steer a ship in such a 'perfect' storm.

As the 21st century unfolds, there are four strong winds blowing across the world and converging to create a more than perfect storm which is challenging captains of business and government institutions that are not designed for these conditions.

The first strong wind is the idea of free markets and capitalism. This is not a new idea. Often attributed to Adam Smith, it has been around for at least 200 years. This wind has gathered more strength in the last twenty years, with the name of 'globalization', one of the most often used words in the media in these years.

It is estimated that the ratio of global foreign direct investment (FDI)—which is investment across national borders—was 25 per cent of world GDP in 2006, five times larger than it was a quarter of a century earlier. As a share of global output, trade between countries is now at almost three times the level in the 1950s.

With the spread of free markets everywhere, and into India too with the opening of our economy in the 1990s, the economies of many countries have been growing faster. Most noteworthy is the growth of China and India, both with over a billion people. The growth in their economies is enabling many millions of people to escape poverty.

Economic growth in free markets follows the principle of cumulative causation. As the market is opened up, those who already have some assets—financial, educational or access to political power—can take advantage of the opportunities available. And their incomes and wealth grows faster than that of those who do not have these assets. Thus economic growth in freer markets is accompanied by increases in gaps of income and wealth. So it is no surprise that the Gini coefficient (which is a measure of the inequality of incomes) is increasing in China, Russia, India, and in other countries that have embraced the free market and capitalism. In time, the benefits of economic growth trickle down to the poorer people when they begin to acquire access to education, finance and employment opportunities.

In this model, one must be patient. And, in this model, to force redistribution is 'socialist' and wrong. On the other hand, to induce the rich to accelerate the growth of their assets, by giving them tax breaks, so that the economy can become larger, is capitalist and acceptable.

The second wind that has been gaining strength across the world is respect for the rights of all human beings—white or black, male or female, rich or poor. This is a more recent force than capitalism. Indeed, many countries, such as the US, that have been stoutly capitalist for centuries, have only in the last fifty years addressed the rights of large sections of their populations, for example, the blacks in the US.

This force, of respecting the rights of all, combines well with the idea of democracy. It has been gaining a lot of strength in the last two decades, with the collapse of the totalitarian governments in the erstwhile Soviet Union and the revolutions of the Arab Spring. Blowing around deep within this second strong wind is the notion of justice, equity and fairness. From the perspective of economists there may be nothing wrong with disparities increasing as economies grow. It is part of the game, they may say. But is it fair from a human perspective? ask others.

The third is the voice of the planet we inhabit, giving us signals in many ways, cautioning us that we are straining it too much. Now everyone is becoming concerned about the state of the environment. We all agree that the paradigm of economic growth that has brought the rich countries their wealth is not sustainable. Mankind's global footprint—which is a measure of the pressure human activity exerts on the resources of the earth—was 60 per cent of the earth's capacity to renew itself in 1960. It has now reached 130 per cent of the earth's capacity. We are no longer living off the revenue account; we are eating into our natural capital.

The US's footprint on the earth's resources is as heavy as 9.7 hectares per person. Europe and Japan's footprints are half of that—4.7 hectares per person. China's is one-sixth of the US—1.6 hectares per person. And India's is half of China's—0.8 hectares per person. So an Indian consumes one-twelfth of the earth's resources compared to an American. Scientists project that if India and China, which will consume more of the earth's resources as their economies grow, were to have a global footprint equal to Japan's by 2030—which is half of the US's present footprint—then these two countries' economies will require another whole planet earth to support them alone. But we have only one earth to share amongst the rich countries and the poorer ones.

The fourth wind, of more recent origin, is the gale force of information. Within the last twenty years, telecommunications and the Internet have enabled people to reach out and be reached in a way that is unprecedented in human history. This wind has become a Category 6 storm. You can now instantly make a call to anywhere in the world using a mobile phone. Twenty years ago you could not do this. Not even in the US. Today mobile phones are accessible even to the poor, across India and in other countries too. The use of mobile phones is accelerating rapidly. In 2004, there were 5.4 billion mobile subscribers in the world. By 2012 the number increased to 6.8 billion according to the International Telecommunication Union, which is over 90 per cent of the world's population.

Today, the Internet and various search engines, of which Google is the most popular, can provide information on almost anything. This was not possible fifteen years ago. In 1996, there were sixteen million users of the Internet in the world, only 0.40 per cent of the world's population. By 2013, the number increased to 2.75 billion users, 38.8 per cent of the world's population. Facebook, which came into existence only in 2004, already has a billion subscribers. Thus people's eyes and ears have been opened to the condition of the world and to the condition of their lives in relation to others in ways that were not possible till even a few years ago.

With these four storm winds converging a more than perfect storm has formed. With information flowing around and many more voices being heard, two major concerns have arisen about the way the world is progressing. One is about sustaining economic growth—'Our pattern of economic growth is not sustainable'—and the other is about fairness in economic growth—'Our pattern of economic growth is not fair'.

These concerns are putting pressure for reform in institutions of capitalism, government and democracy so that economic growth can be more sustainable, more inclusive, and more fair.

THE RUMBLING EARTHQUAKE

My first image was the more than perfect storm, with the four forces converging in the 21st century, putting pressure on institutions. My second image is a rumbling earthquake, with institutions of capitalism, democracy and government grating against each other like three tectonic plates. The misalignment amongst these plates is creating tremors in global governance.

Thomas Friedman, in his book *The World is Flat* (2005), said that the world has been flattened by the force of global trade and international businesses spreading across the world, fuelled by new technologies. Countries, competing for FDI from MNCs, are accelerating the spread of MNCs. Friedman says that companies have never had more freedom and less friction in the way they operate. He points out that the biggest source of friction has always been the nation-state, with its clearly defined boundaries and laws. He says what this will mean for the long-term relationship between companies and the country in which they are headquartered is simply unclear.

The second plate then is the world of nations with their boundaries and their governments. There are many tensions within national governments with demands to improve justice within their national boundaries. At the same time, attempts to create democratic forms of governance that cross national boundaries are under strain too. The EU is greatly stressed. The WTO is spluttering along. International negotiations to create a global regime for governance of the environment have gone from Rio through Kyoto, Bali, Copenhagen, Durban, to Rio again twenty years later without having gone anywhere.

MNCs and global finance float above the plate of national governments and cross national boundaries. A deeper tectonic plate within the earth, also cutting across national boundaries, is communities of identity. The roots of many communities go back into history and traditions, predating by centuries the present national boundaries that have either divided such communities or sought to contain them. Across the world, there are communities that are divided by national boundaries, for example, in Korea, China-Taiwan, India-Pakistan, Northern Ireland, Israel-Palestine, Sudan, and the Kurds in Iraq, Syria and Turkey. At the same time, there are many communities within the national boundaries whose historical roots require special attention—the Basques in Spain, the Tamils in Sri Lanka, communities within Nigeria, multiple communities within India (in the Northeast, the tribal communities within the heartland, etc.). The list goes on.

Friedman's earlier book, *The Lexus and the Olive Tree* (1999), written before 9/11, described two forces in contention. The Lexus represented the forces of global business and global brands. The olive tree represented the 'fundamentalist' forces of tradition, religion and identity. He was convinced then that it was only a matter of time and that the force of the Lexus would wipe out the olive tree. However, he did not realize how deep-rooted the olive tree is. The events of 9/11 were a wake-up call. The olive tree reacted to being smothered, using the same forces of technology that are supposedly flattening the world, to strike back at the Empire. The terrorists used the Internet, mobile phones, UPS and commercial airliners in their strike that flattened the World Trade Center.

The Indian peepul tree is also very strong. Carelessly leave a seed in the water in which concrete is mixed and a peepul tree will break through the concrete after the house is built. Plaster over it again and the shoots will reappear, as I observed in my little rooftop apartment in Pune, where a peepul kept emerging regardless of the technology I used to suppress it.

Our identities are like deep and strongly rooted trees. Attempts to smother them and anything that hurts or insults them will be strongly resisted and can provoke violent reactions.

The plate of government sits in the fault line between the plates of capitalism (above) and democracy (below). The world will keep shaking as these three tectonic plates grate against each other until a new system of governance can be developed to align them.

The storm of the four forces is swirling in India. With its economic reforms since the 1980s, India joined the world of global trade and finance just when, with the fall of the former Soviet Union, ideas of an open, free market and capitalist economies had claimed an ideological victory. Concepts of democracy and human rights have been built into India's Constitution and its political discourse since its independence from colonial rulers in the middle of the last century. A noisy and free media in the country has been supplemented by communications over mobile phones and Internet-enabled social media. India, with its 1.2 billion people—expected to grow to 1.5 billion even—may be the most environmentally stressed large country in the world—for fresh water, land and green cover to meet the needs of its growing population and growing economy.

Institutions that were designed for the 19th and 20th centuries therefore cannot withstand the pressures of the more than perfect storm and the earthquake in the 21st century. They must be redesigned.

2

INDIA IN TRANSITION

The romance of democracy is that somehow the result will come out the way you want, but everything we know about democracy is that the result comes out the way the people want.

—JOHN MUELLER

India is a hotspot for the convergence of the four forces that are combining to shake up institutions in all countries.

In 1991, India made some watershed economic reforms when its balance of payments deficit became unsustainable. It reduced import duties and opened up its economy to global trade. Controls on industrial enterprises, on what they can produce, how much of it and where, similar to the Soviet model of planning, which had stifled the private sector until the 1980s, were dismantled. With these changes India joined the global economy in ideological spirit and practice too. India's merchandise trade has increased from 12.7 per cent of its gross domestic product (GDP) in 1990 to 42.5 per cent in 2012. Foreign direct investment (FDI) had increased from only 0.07 per cent of its GDP in 1990 to 3.55 per cent by 2008 before the global financial crisis.

The force of democracy has been very strong in India for much longer. It was nurtured by the leaders of India's freedom movement, especially Mahatma Gandhi for whom freedom meant freedom from oppression of Indians by other Indians too. These principles of equality are enshrined in independent India's Constitution. In India, the wider opening of the economy to the ideas of free markets and capitalism encountered an entrenched democracy. The fact that India granted all its citizens equal voting rights even before the United States (US) granted them to its black citizens is well known. Less well known perhaps is the growth of non-governmental organizations (NGOs) in India. India has possibly the largest number of active non-government, not-for-profit organizations in the world. A recent study by the Indian government counted 3.3 million of them: one for every 400 Indians! Many of these are engaged in service delivery and many are noisy, unputdownable, defenders of citizens' rights.

While the West describes environmental problems as an impending environmental crisis that is expected within the next few decades due to global warming by excess carbon accumulations in the atmosphere, Indians are already facing an acute environmental problem. India is turning out to be amongst the more water-scarce countries in the world. Presently described only as 'water stressed' rather than 'water scarce', the trends are alarming. As it is large numbers of people do not have access to adequate quantities of clean water for drinking and sanitation. Indeed, this is one of the principal causes for the persistent levels of poor health and stunted growth of Indian children (often described as a problem of 'malnutrition'). With the country's economic growth and growing population, a 50 per cent gap is estimated between current supply and projected demand for water. Moreover, nine out of twenty of the country's river basins are already facing water scarcity and groundwater levels in the country are falling rapidly as farmers and city-dwellers have taken to bore deeper and deeper to meet their water requirements. Per capita water availability decreased from 2,309 cubic metres in 1991 to 1,588 cubic metres in 2001, and is projected to decrease further to only 1,000 cubic metres in 2025 which would be termed as a water scarcity situation. For Indians, the impact of environmental degradation is being faced acutely here and now in terms of increasing water scarcity. Therefore, the impact of increasing levels of carbon in the atmosphere (and that too caused by the developed economies), which will begin to effect the world in the next few decades according to climate scientists (which is a principal environmental issue for the West), is a secondary problem for Indians.

There has been an explosion of Indian citizens' access to information in the last fifteen years. India has over 700 million mobile phone users. Poor Indians, even in remote villages, use mobile phones. The number of regional television (TV) news channels has increased from just three in 2000 to eighty-two (in 2010). Overall, India has one of the largest numbers—around 150—of TV news channels in the world today. India's Right to Information (RTI) Act of 2005, a landmark legislation, has enabled these channels, and also India's ubiquitous NGOs mentioned earlier, to create a veritable maelstrom with information to stir up people's passions on various issues. These include concerns about inequality, the destruction of the environment and corruption.

Conditions in India today are vastly different to what they were when India became independent in 1947. Conditions in India in 2013 are very different to what they were even fifteen years ago on account of the storm created by the coming together of the four forces that are shaking up global institutions. India's government sits on the fault line where the forces of globalization and capitalism meet strong democratic forces within the country.

A ship sailing through uncertain conditions would do well to have a navigator with the right tools for navigation. Following India's independence from British rule in 1947, the country adopted a parliamentary system of government and a federal structure.

India's first prime minister, the far-sighted Jawaharlal Nehru, added a Planning Commission in 1950. While his cabinet, which he chaired as prime minister, had to be formed from elected Members of Parliament (MPs), the Planning Commission, which he would also chair, would consist of experts chosen by the prime minister himself.

The Planning Commission would look ahead and prepare five year plans for the development of the country and recommend allocation of resources to the central cabinet and to the state governments too. Forward planning is required by organizations, small and large, to steer themselves, including business corporations and business conglomerates. Forward planners are the navigators. They must choose the instruments they will use, of which there are many.

Early on, India's planners adopted mathematical models of inputs and outputs to map the economy and to direct its plans. Therefore, the Planning Commission was mostly staffed with statisticians and economists. This model of planning was similar to the Soviet model of central planning. The centre directed the plans of the various ministries and states by the allocations it made to them and by approving their plans. This model had driven the preparation of all of India's earlier five year plans since 1951 and it lingers on even today.

Over sixty years have passed since the creation of India's Planning Commission. What India needs now is another approach to planning, one that fits the challenges of the new India. The new India is no longer ruled by a single, dominant party at the centre and in the states, as was the case with the Congress when the Planning Commission was formed by Jawaharlal Nehru to advise the government. Another substantial change that has taken place with the economic reforms since the late 1980s is that the private sector now has a much larger role in the economy and government investments a lesser role. Therefore, financial allocations by the Planning Commission do not matter for growth as much as they used to. The consequence of these changes is that the central government is not in a position to impose its will on the states and on the private sector as it once did.

At the same time, the new configuration of the Indian economy and Indian politics is throwing up new challenges. The advent of coalition governments at the centre and regional parties in the states makes coordination of actions more difficult. Private investments into the priorities of the country can no longer be controlled by government permissions. Nevertheless, huge challenges of development remain and some way has to be found to direct scarce resources towards national priorities. How do you obtain alignment amongst the many actors in a system you do not have the power to command? This requires a new vision of planning.

SCENARIO PLANNING

My friend Montek Singh Ahluwalia was appointed a member of the Planning Commission in 1999. I was intrigued about what Montek would do. He had served many years in the World Bank. When he came back to India he was a close advisor to Prime Minister Rajiv Gandhi in the freeing of the economy from central controls that Rajiv Gandhi initiated. Thereafter Montek, along with Finance Minister Manmohan Singh and Commerce Minister Chidambaram, was a member of the team that assisted Prime Minister Narasimha Rao in the reforms of 1991 that dismantled the edifice of industrial licensing and controls and opened up the Indian economy to foreign trade too.

I wrote to Montek from the US where I was consulting at that time. My consulting practice was focused on systems of strategic planning in conditions of uncertainty and on assisting large organizations to bring about transformational change. I asked Montek what he expected to do in the Planning Commission, which continued as a central planning body, inconsistent with his beliefs that such organizations must be dismantled to free the economy. I mentioned to him that other methods of planning were being developed and applied, very different to the Soviet-style centralized control model that seemed to continue to drive India's approach to planning. One such new approach, I mentioned in my letter, was scenario planning and amongst the examples I mentioned to him was the Mont Fleur scenarios that had been developed in South Africa a few years earlier. Montek was intrigued.

South Africa was being torn apart in the early 1990s. The blacks and whites were in violent conflict. Amongst the blacks were deep political divisions. How would all the warring parties come together to plan the future of South Africa? A small group of South Africans, white and black, political persons and businessmen, came together to analyse what the future of South Africa could be depending on the path its politics and its economy would follow. They developed four alternative scenarios of South Africa's future using the techniques of 'scenario planning'. These scenarios showed in numbers and in pictures that people could comprehend the consequences of following the different paths. Thus people from all walks of life, in towns and in villages, could be engaged in a large, national conversation about what they would like South Africa to become, and the policies the people must support to shape the future they want.

Montek suggested I try this new approach in India. Montek moved to the International Monetary Fund (IMF) while I returned to India in 2000 and, with the help of my friend, Tarun Das, director general of the Confederation of Indian Industry (CII), enrolled others to develop scenarios for India. Many Indians from different walks of life came together to try out this new approach for creating a strategy for their country. This exercise produced deep insights into India's challenges and pointed to ways in which they could be addressed. It called for a new approach to leadership and collaboration.

The inputs for these scenarios were provided by many people who listened to each other's aspirations and suggestions. These people included politicians, business leaders, civil society activists and academicians. They also included women from villages in Haryana, weavers from Karnataka, college students from the Indian Institutes of Technology (IITs), and even homeless children who lived on the streets outside the New Delhi railway station. All of us, rich and poor, young and old, were Indians. We were all equal under our Constitution. India is often compared to an elephant. And a story is often told about how several blind men around an elephant had to each say what they could feel when they touched the elephant—one the leg, another the tail, and a third the trunk. Only by putting their impressions together could they understand what the animal really was. Similarly, many perspectives must be brought together to understand India. This proper understanding is necessary before one can make viable plans for India's progress.

India is not a set of economic numbers. India is a billion human beings with hopes and aspirations. Their aspirations must shape the objectives of the plan. Therefore planners must listen to the people. It is difficult to listen to diverse people because they do not always agree. But listen we must. Therefore, planning for a diverse country which has enshrined equality in its democratic Constitution requires that planners find a way to listen to the people. Planning in India has to change from 'telling' the states, the private sector and the people what they should do, to shaping plans with the states, the private sector and the people. Democracy is government of the people, for the people, and by the people.

Therefore, in democratic India, planning for the people must be by the people too.

This requires an innovative approach. Scenario planning provides a set of tools with interesting possibilities. When I returned to India in 2000, I got many opportunities to work with NGOs and business associations on challenges such as malnutrition, slum renewal and innovative approaches to improve education for the poor. Those were the years when India's GDP growth had begun to accelerate. Economists had begun to project India as one of the world's three giant economies, along with China and the US, by 2040. Indian business people, economists and policymakers were in a celebratory mood. India was shining. The future was ours.

However some people were sceptical. They pointed out that economists' projections have an awful track record because they do not factor into their models the social and political forces that can change the trajectory of their economic extrapolations. They pointed out that in the early 1980s economists were comparing the US and the Soviet Union as the two largest economic blocs. And economists were expecting Japan to be the powerful economy of the 21st century—they even talked of a Japanese century. China did not even figure in their projections then. Yet, within fifteen years, the picture changed dramatically. There was no Soviet Union and Japan was in the doldrums. Instead, China was the emergent power of the 21st century! So, how could one be sure of India's future trajectory? Did economists really understand what was going on within India, including the socio-political forces which would influence India's future?

The World Economic Forum (WEF) undertook to apply the techniques of scenario planning in 2005 to examine the future of the BRICs countries—China, Brazil, Russia and India. The forum's scenarists asked me to help them. The insights that had already been produced by the participative scenario exercise conducted in India previously proved invaluable in understanding what the future of India could be.

THREE SCENARIOS

Three scenarios emerged about India's future. The first scenario was called BollyWorld (a spoof on 'Bollywood', the popular name for India's prolific movie industry). It was a combination of two worlds that were growing side by side in India. These worlds were described in pictures. One was a picture of peacocks strutting with little birds scrambling around them for grain. This was the story of the opening of markets in India. The goal of economic reforms is to improve the lives of the poorest people. Thus, in this picture, the courtyard is opened and grains are scattered for the birds to eat. The hope is that the little sparrows will get the grains. However, the pigeons are stronger and they get to the grains first. And when the peacock arrives, even the pigeons move aside. They will have to wait till the peacock has fed. This scenario portrays what happens when markets are opened. Those who already have the wherewithal to take advantage of new opportunities, who have some capital, or good education, or access to people in power, will get the benefits of opportunities first. Thus they will become richer and stronger. Others cannot access the opportunities as easily and so disparities in incomes grow. The rich show off their new wealth, the big cars they drive, the branded clothes they wear, and the huge mansions they live in. They are the peacocks.

However, there exists another vivid picture in the BollyWorld scenario. It is a picture of wolves prowling in the jungle. A picture of spreading violence in many districts of the country, and even in India's cities, side by side with the show of wealth. According to the WEF's scenarists, this combination of glamour and violence was like a Bollywood movie. In this scenario, India was becoming a BollyWorld. Good fun to watch from the outside but increasingly dangerous on the inside. A world that was not sustainable.

The tensions within, and the political reactions to them, could result in the second scenario called Atakta Bharat ('India stalling'). The picture describing this scenario had buffaloes wallowing in a pond, with a little boy waiting outside. The buffaloes represent senior netas (leaders) holding important offices, and experts in many fields, who are expected to develop and implement plans to shape the future of the country. Such plans should produce results for the people, especially our children (represented by the boy waiting outside the pond) who are the future of the country. The netas and experts are expected to develop and implement plans for the future of the country. However they cannot agree with each other. When one buffalo gets an idea and wants to move ahead, the others do not want to move. So the buffalo settles into the pond again. Then another buffalo gets an idea. But the first remembers that he had not received cooperation and so reciprocates by refusing to cooperate! Thus decisions are not made and progress is stalled. Meanwhile, the children of the country are waiting for education to be improved, and for health care and nutrition.

These scenarios were created in 2005. They predicted that BollyWorld could slip into Atakta Bharat. Fortunately, signs of another scenario of India were also emerging like little shoots of grass. It was observed that there were many local initiatives, and many entrepreneurs, that were improving their own conditions and the lives of the people around them. Though each of these initiatives may be small, their numbers were multiplying. Women self-help groups (SHGs), community water management programmes, producers' cooperatives, grass-roots innovators, millions of small scale enterprises—these bottom-up initiatives were transforming lives wherever they were lit up. This scenario of 'Fireflies Arising' and lighting up the darkness represented a changing India. The WEF scenarists called this scenario 'Pahale India' ('India first') because this was the process by which a democratic and diverse India would become the first. A big power lit up by millions of fireflies.

The WEF commissioned two economic forecasting groups, the National Council of Applied Economic Research (NCAER) in India and the Oxford Forecasting Group in the United Kingdom (UK), to evaluate the scenarios in economic terms. The forecasters confirmed that while both BollyWorld and Pahale India would grow the economy to over 9 per cent GDP growth, BollyWorld would not be sustainable. It would deteriorate into Atakta Bharat and growth rates would fall. On the other hand, fireflies of Pahale India was a sustainable model of high growth. Moreover, poverty rates would fall fastest in the Pahale India scenario since more people would be creating the growth. It would be a trickle-up and not a trickle-down process. These scenarios, which were made by citizens of the country in an unofficial exercise, pointed to a sustainable approach for India's inclusive growth.

REFORMING THE PLANNING COMMISSION

Meanwhile, the Planning Commission's official processes moved along as before. In 2009, the Congress party led United Progressive Alliance (UPA)-II came to power. The prime minister, Dr Manmohan Singh, who chaired the Planning Commission, invited me to join the commission as a member. Montek Ahluwalia had returned to India and now was the deputy chairman of the Planning Commission. The prime minister and Montek asked me to consider how the overall process of planning could be reformed.

They gave me a list of twenty respected citizens of the country.

Some of these individuals have worked in government in very senior positions, some even in the Planning Commission in the past, and some are respected industrialists of the country. I asked each of these twenty leaders three questions:

- Is the Planning Commission playing a useful role for the country?
- If not, is there another role that the Planning Commission could play in India's progress?
- In what way could the commission transform itself to play this role?

The answer to the first question was unanimous. The Planning Commission was no longer making a significant contribution to the progress of the country. The country had changed. It was more decentralized, both politically and administratively. The private sector was playing an increasingly large role. The Indian economy was more connected with the international economy. For all these reasons, the five year plans, made by some experts in Delhi and which had to be implemented by people across the country, were not very useful.

However, everyone, including the industrialists, said that the dynamic nature of the changes in India and outside required that there be a strategic group that, like a radar, could sense the forces that were causing change to happen and that could provide governments in the centre and in the states, and private industry too, with insights into the forces shaping the future. These national thought leaders wanted the Planning Commission to lift itself out of the rut of allocating funds and approving proposals and play a much more strategic role in helping to shape the future. To many the Planning Commission's experts were like 'the buffaloes wallowing in the pond', while India's children were waiting for results. Our children need better education, health care and sanitation, and jobs to be created much faster, so that they can provide the demographic dividend to our economy.

A NEW BEGINNING

If the people of the country and the politicians they elect have to support the plans, and also play a role in their implementation, then it is necessary that people understand the plans. Perhaps they must also participate in shaping the plans. Therefore, the Planning Commission changed its approach when making the 12th Five Year Plan. This time round, much more input was obtained from people across the country, especially those groups who feel they are not sufficiently included in the plans.

To begin with, the Planning Commission's 200 officers worked in cross-disciplinary teams to distil twelve systemic challenges facing the country, including how to make markets more equitable and efficient and how to make access to information more democratic. The commission invited civil society organizations that represent all those who have not been sufficiently included in the progress of the country: the tribals, dalits, minorities, urban poor, and physically challenged, among others. They were asked to consider these systemic challenges, to consult their constituents around the country, and bring back to the Planning Commission the voices of the people. Thus 950 civil society organizations were involved, and through them the voices of millions must have been heard. At the same time, business associations were also asked to consider these twelve challenges, to consult their members and bring forward their suggestions. Expert groups and think tanks gave their suggestions too. The challenges were also posted on the Internet and Facebook, and thousands of responses were received.

The Approach to the 12th Five Year Plan was drafted. This draft was discussed with the state governments in five regional conclaves in which their views were sought. In these conclaves, representatives of local governments—panchayats and urban local bodies or ULBs—also participated and gave their perspectives. With all these inputs, a final Approach was written, and approval obtained from the National Development Council, in which the chief ministers of all the states participated.

Many hundreds of people participated in the preparation of the 12th Five Year Plan, a large number of whom were civil society organizations representing the many segments of India's people who have not been sufficiently included in India's growth so far nor included in the past in the process of planning the country's growth. They had great hope that the more inclusive process adopted for the 12th Plan would result in a more inclusive strategy. However, when they saw the drafts of the plan they were very disappointed. The 12th Five Year Plan resembled previous plans; the people's voices were missing. The official planning process appeared to have fallen into a rut again.

Representatives of some of these organizations requested a meeting with the deputy chairman and members of the Planning Commission to express their disappointment. The deputy chairman expressed his inability to change the direction of the plans at that stage. The dialogue broke down. I suggested to the civil society leaders that we conduct a new process that ran parallel with the official process. We could use the techniques of scenario planning that are more inclusive and more systemic, and could produce descriptions of strategies that would be much easier for citizens to understand than the language and numbers used in conventional plans. Some of these leaders were familiar with the insightful and evocative Mont Fleur scenarios created in South Africa in the 1990s. They agreed to participate in the process. The deputy chairman also agreed with the proposition of a parallel process that would supplement the official plans.

After this meeting, many people with diverse backgrounds came together to develop scenarios of India's future to facilitate new, collaborative conversations amongst citizens and policymakers about India's future. They were aided in their efforts by the Center for Study of Science, Technology and Policy (CSTEP) which developed the conceptual scenarios model into a more robust system dynamics model.

The purpose of 'scenario thinking' is to project the 'what if' angle. *What if* we do not change our underlying theories-in-use about progress and governance? On the other hand, *what if* we begin to adopt alternative theories to guide our progress? Scenarios are projections of plausible outcomes of alternative courses of action. They can help us choose the strategies that can produce the outcomes we want. Scenarios also enable dialogues, which can lead to agreements.

THE SYSTEM MODEL

Inputs were obtained from many diverse people and sources of information, as mentioned before, to understand the forces that were impacting India's growth. The relationship between the fundamental forces that emerged from the systems analysis is presented in Figure 2.1.

The analysis locates the leverage points: the forces that affect the condition of all others. These lie in the design of institutions (seen in the middle of Figure 2.1). The architecture of governance has an impact on trust in government institutions and large businesses. Business models directly affect science and innovations, which in turn have an impact on the sustainability of the earth's resources. Lack of trust in institutions increases impatience in society and this leads to a political logjam which in turn makes reforms that the system needs more difficult.

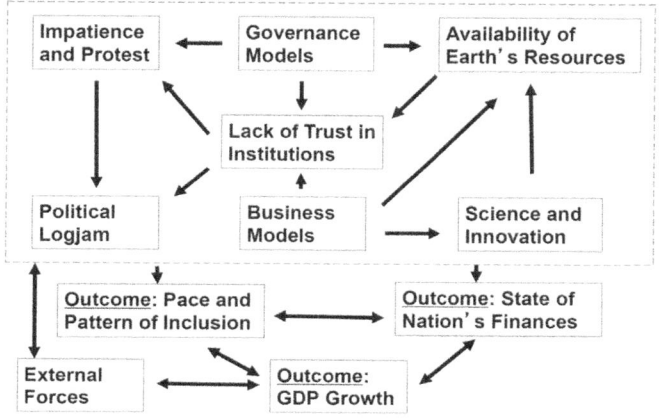

Figure 2.1: Root Causes and Leverage Points

The condition of the system and its ability to reform itself will determine the pace and pattern of inclusion in growth. It will also affect the state of the nation's finances. Therefore, predictions of GDP growth rates must be related to the condition of the system and the social, political and institutional forces within it, which are often treated as exogenous to economic growth models. Finally, the condition of external factors that impact India's progress is not easy to forecast. Therefore, the most important question for the country's policymakers is: what strategy will ensure that the country will be best placed regardless of these external uncertainties? Not surprisingly, India will be most secure in times of uncertainty if it is internally cohesive and strong. Therefore, when the world around is changing, the plan for India must concentrate even more on institutional reforms within.

Reforms in the processes of governance, administration and implementation are the need of the hour. India's 12th Five Year Plan has incorporated 'scenario planning' for the first time, presenting the three scenarios, and recognizing that development and growth outcomes will depend on the extent to which we are able to take difficult decisions.

THREE FORKS IN THE ROAD TO THE FUTURE

Many of the strong forces that will shape our future, like the demographics of India and the spread of communications with new technologies, are 'givens'. However, other forces that will strongly shape our future are not necessarily givens. The future shape of the system—the quality of the inclusion as well as the financial condition of the economy—will depend on the choices we make.

Like an X-ray, the analysis of the system shows a deeper pattern. When we make certain choices, many other forces that depend on them will change accordingly. And, when they go another way, another 'scenario' altogether can emerge. It is not surprising that the three fundamental forces located by the system's analysis that can shape India's future are about approaches to development and governance.

A. The approach we take to 'inclusion': The what and the how of inclusion

A principal challenge for economists and policymakers all over the world has become how to achieve 'inclusion' along with economic growth. Two contending approaches are evident. One emphasizes 'redistribution': taking from those who have more, and giving to those who do not have enough. The other approach emphasizes creating more access to opportunities, so that the less well-off can increase their incomes faster and also contribute to growing the pie. At one extreme, the emphasis is mostly on 'handouts'. At the other extreme is a very determined effort to generate more opportunities for livelihood and to provide all sections of society with access to opportunities. Scenarios can project the consequences of choosing one course over the other.

B. The approach we take to 'governance': Will we strengthen local, community-based and collaborative governance rapidly?

When systems seem to be 'not in control', the instinct is to centralize. However, if the reasons for slow results are that the diversity in the system is very large and therefore solutions must be locally adapted, and that there is not a capable centre, then it may be best to strengthen local governance rather than try to impose central control. The need to break across the silos and create convergence has been recognized.

At one extreme, the way most things are run is, in effect, 'central' and 'siloed'. At the other, local rural and urban governments are effectively in charge of their affairs with vigorous participation of local citizens. In a devolved structure with power closer to where results are required, and with different parts of the system working collaboratively, adaptation and learning are faster too.

C. The 'theory-in-use' towards energy and environmental solutions (as well as enterprises): Big projects or more community-based solutions and enterprises?

Local and smaller solutions can create more ownership and responsibility for the use of resources and also ensure more equity in distribution of benefits. The argument against this theory is that scale is required for more efficiency. Innovations in networked enterprise designs can enable the benefits of both, local ownership as well as the benefit of scale where required. On one end, big is good is the dominant paradigm. At the other end, only small is beautiful.

THREE SCENARIOS OF INDIA'S FUTURE

The analysis of the system reveals three scenarios of India. They can be described under the headings 'Muddling Along' (or Insufficient Action) 'Falling Apart' (or Policy Logjam) and 'The Flotilla Advances' (or Strong, Inclusive Growth). These scenarios result from three different configurations of the three 'theories-in-use' outlined previously.

Each scenario is an explanation of the system it depicts (the country in this case) if the forces that affect it play out, or are caused to play out, in one way rather than another. Internal consistency requires that implausible combinations of directions of the forces are not considered. The India scenarios are constructed around the leverage points in the more fundamental forces explained above. They are derived from an analysis of all the critical forces identified in the scenario process. Thus, the scenarios are comprehensive and internally consistent descriptions of different states of the country's future. The NCAER was commissioned to create a macroeconomic model and project the quantitative outcomes of the scenarios.

Scenario 1: The Flotilla Advances

This is an optimistic scenario under the assumption that the government would successfully drive key structural policy reforms and their effective implementation. Decentralization and good governance policies will improve the efficiency of the public delivery system and address the supply side bottlenecks. Under a positive policy environment, the investment climate would also be positive, with significant net capital inflows and healthy growth in private investment, both being drivers of economic growth.

Reforms in oil, fertilizers and other key sectors would improve the fiscal position of the government. Subsidies, particularly oil and fertilizer subsidies, will be phased out substantially during the

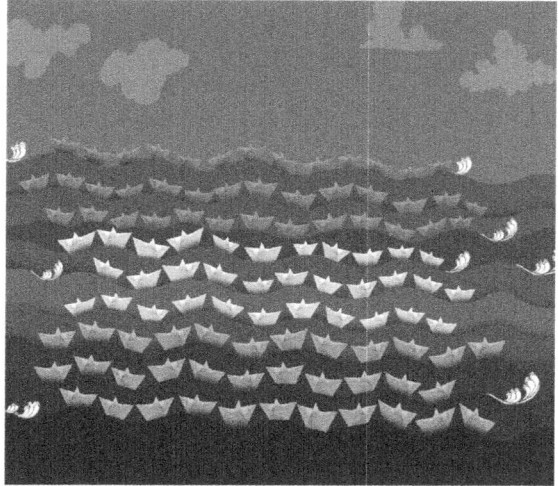

Figure 2.2: Flotilla Advances

12th Plan period, amounting to 1.4 per cent of GDP by 2016–17. Fiscal consolidation not only depends on cutting down unproductive expenditure like subsidies and interest payments, but also on expanding the tax base and improving revenue collection. The implementation of Direct Taxes Code (DTC) and Goods and Services Tax (GST) would improve tax collection from 2014–15 onwards.

The government diverts a part of these fiscal savings towards creating more productive assets, including improving human capital. Increased allocations to health and education sectors are expected to improve the quality of human resources and raise GDP growth in the long term.

Under this scenario, the government is able to meet its medium-term fiscal goals, with the deficit coming down to around 3.6 per cent of GDP by 2015–16 from the current level of 5 per cent of GDP.

The overall GDP at constant 2004–5 prices is projected to

grow by an average of 7.8 per cent during the 12th Plan period (reaching 9.3 per cent by 2016–17). Across the production sectors, the services sector is expected to register higher growth of 9 per cent followed by the industry sector at around 7.1 per cent and the agriculture sector at 3.3 per cent.

Scenario 2: Muddling Along

Under this scenario, India would initiate some reform measures to encourage investment. However, the business environment continues to remain weak as the reforms may cover only a narrow set of issues. Net invisible receipts and FDI inflows will remain weak due to domestic policy uncertainty. The stock market (BSE Sensex) will continue to show poor returns in this scenario and there will be more pressure on the rupee to depreciate against the US dollar. Both central and state governments will miss the opportunities to control unproductive expenditure.

Figure 2.3: Muddling Along

The overall GDP growth is estimated at 6.0 per cent per year for the 12th Plan period, a decline of 1.8 percentage points over the Flotilla Advances scenario. The decline in GDP growth has occurred in the services and industry sectors due to decline of private investment in these non-agriculture sectors. There is also less impact on poverty reduction as the growth effects are smaller.

Scenario 3: Falling Apart

This is the most pessimistic scenario among the three, both in terms of economic performance and policy environment. This scenario reflects a situation where the government would be unable to undertake key policy reforms. Subsidy levels are not stabilized. The policy logjam, especially relating to investments, witnessed in the latter part of the 11th Five Year Plan would continue. The tax revenue growth will remain weak with the

Figure 2.4: Falling Apart

implementation of key tax policy reforms, such as DTC and GST, being delayed further.

The allocation of resources in the health and education sectors would decline as a ratio to GDP from the current levels due to resource constraints. The public sector investment both in agriculture and non-agriculture sectors would decline substantially as compared to the pre-crisis level.

The overall annual GDP growth for the 12th Plan is estimated at 4.8 per cent, a decline of 3 percentage points over the Flotilla Advances scenario. The GDP growth rate declines across all the sectors because of significant fall of investment (both private and public) and a rising fiscal deficit. The country will enter the 'low-middle income growth trap'. The results also show high fiscal and current account deficits, which are unsustainable as the debt levels would rise, leading to greater debt servicing burden. Significant decline of GDP growth would also jeopardize the inclusiveness of growth, and poverty reduction will be much smaller than in the Flotilla Advances scenario.

Some principal macroeconomic outcomes of the three scenarios from NCAER's analysis are given in Table 2.1.

Table 2.1:
Major Outcomes by Fifth Year of 12th Plan (FY 2016–17)

	Pace of Inclusion (Poverty Ratio)	GDP Growth	Fiscal Deficit
Flotilla Advances	21.7%	9.3%	3.0%
Muddling Along	22.8%	6.5%	4.0%
Falling Apart	24.2%	5.0%	4.5%

INDIA AT A TURNING POINT: WHICH SCENARIO WILL EMERGE?

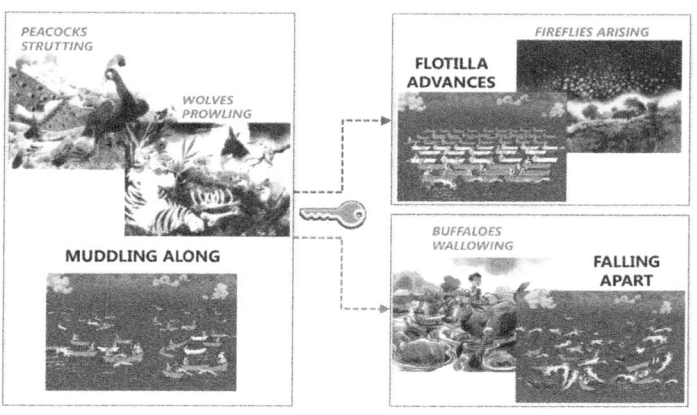

India is currently described as Muddling Along. If we now focus on implementing the overdue governance reforms, we can expect a speeding up of the India flotilla's progress and cohesion. If we do not implement governance and institutional reforms very soon, we can expect a further falling apart of the system and the India growth story.

Figure 2.5: The Keys to Produce the Scenario We Want

Planners cannot create a spirit of shared vision in citizens: they can only provide paths and plans for realization of the vision. At most, they may provide a seed to start conversations about a shared vision for India's future.

The scenarios, along with the system analysis of forces and elements of an emerging vision, provide starting points for a new conversation between the Planning Commission and stakeholders, and also amongst citizens. There is no guarantee that this process will result in a consensus. But it is certain that in the absence of a good dialogue about these issues a consensus is even less likely!

Therefore, what is the character of the country that Indians want, and how will they build it together?

The prime minister (and chairman of the Planning Commission), Dr Manmohan Singh, while asking the Planning Commission to reform itself, had directed it to become a 'systems reforms commission' and an 'essay in persuasion'. Scenarios explain the reforms to the system—the 'theories-in-use' and the 'policy matrix'—required to produce faster, more rapidly inclusive and more sustainable growth. However, people must understand the fundamental shifts in policy required and support them, and press the political system for change. Thus, scenario planning is a complement to the traditional planning process and represents an innovation made in the 12th Five Year Plan.

The Planning Commission is no doubt changing. But it must change much faster to fulfil the new role the country needs it to perform. As a 'systems reform commission' it must not merely allocate money to ministries and states. It must facilitate the reforms of institutions and the creation of 21st century institutions. To be 'an essay in persuasion'—a force for persuading people about the reforms they must support—it must listen to the people and speak to them in words and images they understand. This is the new vision of planning for India, a country of millions of points of light and energy. All inspired by a shared vision of the future that people want for themselves and their children.

A GRANDSON'S ADVICE

What sort of world do we want to leave our grandchildren? This is a rhetorical question we often ask. But, what sort of world do our grandchildren want? My grandson lives in the US. When he was five years old, he visited us in Delhi. I drove him around the fine streets of the city. What he noticed were the beggars at the traffic lights, knocking on the car's window for attention. He asked me, 'Why do they have to do everything on the street?' He saw them cooking, eating, sleeping, and trying to earn a living, all on the street. I was not in the government then. He visited us again two years later, now seven years old. He now knew that I was in the government, in the Planning Commission. He looked around Delhi this time and he noticed the beggars still on the streets. He burst out, 'What is the government doing? Counting daisies? Why doesn't it do something for the people?'

That evening he saw a bound copy of the draft Approach to the 12th Five Year Plan on my desk at home. I told him what it was. He said, 'Dadaji (grandfather), what is the use of writing a book. Do something for the people!' My grandson was telling me that the job of the Planning Commission is to make things happen. The Planning Commission's work cannot be just about budgets and numbers—'counting the daisies' as my grandson says.

Planning in India was required to be a participative process, with inputs from the people. However, each five year plan seemed to drift further away from the language and concerns of the people into the realms of economic numbers and financial budgets. Therefore, it has become necessary to adjust the method of planning, to connect planners more strongly with people.

Two questions are being asked with increasing frequency both in India and around the world. Is our pattern of economic growth sustainable? And, is our pattern of growth fair? It is clear that a new approach is required for human development and societal progress. If the prevalent 'theories-in-use' to define progress, manage development and govern societies continue, the risks to the environment and to social harmony are very large.

'If we don't create the future, the present extends itself,' wrote Toni Morrison in the *Song of Solomon*. Plans must inspire people with a shared vision. Plans must provide an analysis of the forces people must understand, and the reforms they must support. Such plans should persuade people to take necessary actions in order to create the future they want for themselves, their children and grandchildren. This is a vision of what the institution of planning must become in a large democratic country that is aspiring for much more inclusive and sustainable growth.

India's children aspire to live, in the not too distant future, in a just society and an economy without poor people. India's citizens are counting on their leaders, as my young grandson tells me, to do what needs to be done now to create this future. The analysis of the forces retarding faster progress in the country, presented in *Figure 2.1: Root Causes and Leverage Points* reveals what they must do. Institutions must be reformed urgently i.e. institutions of governance (political parties, government, and regulators) and institutions of business too.

How are institutions reformed? And, what are institutions? To these questions I now turn.

3

THE RULES OF THE GAME

In a constantly changing world, we need the flexibility that only imperfection provides.

—E.O. WILSON

Institutions matter because institutions enable nations and economies to progress. What are institutions? How are institutions formed? Can institutions be changed? These are questions for this chapter. How institutions can be changed will be explained in subsequent chapters.

WHAT ARE INSTITUTIONS?

Douglass C. North received the Nobel Prize in economics in 1993 for his work on the development of institutions and their role in human progress. North defined institutions as the 'humanly devised constraints that structure political, economic and social interactions'. Constraints, he said, are devised as formal rules (constitutions, laws, property rights) and informal restraints (sanctions, taboos, traditions, codes of conduct).

Norms and codes of conduct are the 'unwritten rules of the game' of societies and organizations. They are often more powerful than the 'written rules', stipulated in laws and organization manuals, with which those responsible for the governance and management of societies and organizations seek to control the behaviour of their organizations' members.

Indeed, the unwritten rule that 'the written rule must always be followed' would distinguish Germans from Indians, for example. Evidence of this is the way in which Indian drivers ignore the dividing lines on roads, traffic signals and even one-way road signs. German drivers will always wait at a traffic light when it is red, even when the road is deserted. They are also most unlikely to drive in the wrong direction on a one-way street because it is a short cut. In contrast, Indians drivers will drive through red lights if there is no cop watching, and will blithely drive in the wrong direction on a one-way street! Germans will respect written rules. Indians are much more likely to ignore them.

HOW ARE INSTITUTIONS FORMED?

The origins of cultures go way back in time and the contents of cultures accumulate layer upon layer over centuries.. The deepest layers of human cultures are created through genetic evolution over millennia. On top of these deep layers are the layers of culture that have evolved with the histories of societies and nations, as explained in this chapter. And above these are the different cultural characteristics of the many institutions and organizations situated within those societies and nations.

Cultures and rules of behaviour are shaped not only by social and political histories, but also by genetic evolution, according to sociobiologist E.O. Wilson. However, he adds that while there is a part of culture that is shaped by genetics, there is also a part that is shaped by other forces. In *The Social Conquest of Earth* (Wilson 2013) he writes:

It is not going too far, I believe, to add that the failure of natural selection to create an independent universal grammar has played a major role in the diversification of culture and, from that flexibility and potential inventiveness, the flowering of human genius.

Institutional cultures evolve over time within societies, nations and organizations. How institutions, codes of conduct and constitutions develop may be illustrated by the contrast between India's and China's histories which have resulted in different attitudes towards personal freedoms vis-à-vis order and stability in society and consequentially different norms and codes of conduct.

Three times in twelve years since AD 2000 the process of scenario planning has been applied to create a systematic description of the forces shaping India, and to find the leverage points for positive change in the country. Diverse and different people were engaged with the process each time. The only two common threads in the three exercises were the principles of the scenario process, and I, as the facilitator. All three times the conclusions were the same about the approach required for rapid, inclusive and sustainable development of the country. Though the insights were expressed in different words and different pictures, the consistency in what they revealed is remarkable.

The scenarios show that the only approach with which India can achieve an outcome of inclusive development is to have an inclusive approach to making development happen. In other words, the means used cannot be different from the ends sought. Two evocative and similar pictures have emerged from the three sets of scenarios. They depict the inclusive process of change that diverse and democratic India must adopt. These images are: a multitude of fireflies arising together, and a flotilla of many boats advancing in the same direction. The metaphor in both pictures is of many independent agents, even very small ones, in charge of their lives, moving towards a shared aspiration. Independence and alignment is the way Indians must progress.

India is too diverse and too vast a country to be commanded from a centre. In its long history, whenever a large empire has grown by application of a strong central force, that empire has soon dissolved. The empire of Ashoka the Great, who ruled India from 269 BCE to 232 BCE, was much larger than present-day India. Ashoka's empire stretched from Afghanistan, and perhaps even parts of Iran in the west, to Bangladesh and Assam in the east, and as far south as northern Kerala. Ashoka conquered this vast land with brutal force. His remorse, when he saw the carnage left behind by his armies in the conquest of Kalinga, and his conversion to the doctrines of Gautama Buddha made him abjure violence all together. The empire fell apart not long after his death.

Aurangzeb, who ruled India from AD 1658 until AD 1707 was the last of the great Mughal emperors. Under him the Mughal Empire grew to its maximum extent. However, his policies also contributed to its dissolution. In the first half of his long reign, though much disliked for his ruthlessness in conquest, Aurangzeb followed the recipe of his great-grandfather, Akbar, of reconciling with the enemies he conquered and giving them honourable positions in his empire. But when, in the latter part of his reign, he became intolerant and more vicious in his suppression of religious and regional opponents as he expanded his empire, he sowed the seeds for its dissolution. The Mughal Empire collapsed a few years after Aurangzeb's death.

Then came the British. They aggregated, through war and treaties, an empire in India that was as widespread as Ashoka's. The manner in which a small number of British citizens in India could impose the authority of the British Crown in distant London on the diverse multitude of India was remarkable. However, Great

Britain could not hold on to its Indian empire for very long when confronted by a rising tide of non-violent demands for self-rule against it led by Mahatma Gandhi.

Self-rule to Mahatma Gandhi meant much more than self-rule of India by Indians. He envisioned a country governed from the grass roots up with bottom-up governance, and not controlled from the top. He was also driven by an aspiration to empower women and Harijans (the lower castes and outcasts of Indian society) to participate equally with others in the governance of their villages and their country. He said that India could never be free even if the British left until those masses of Indians who had for centuries been oppressed by their own countrymen were made free of that oppression. Gandhi's aspiration for a good society was similar to Ashoka's vision, some 2,200 years earlier, of a society in which all living beings were given equal respect.

In 1951, independent India promulgated its Constitution. The Constitution gave all adult Indian citizens, men and women, rich and poor, whatever their religion and caste, an equal vote in shaping the future of their country. In fact, India granted equal voting rights to all its citizens even before the United States (US), who gave its black citizens voting rights later.

Every nation, every society, and even every organization in business or government, or a non-governmental organization (NGO), has its own 'culture', shaped by its history, its stories and its heroes. The norms and beliefs that influence the ways in which their members think and act are the principal elements of the cultures of nations, societies and organizations. The trajectory of India's history, and the values that shaped its vision of its future in the run up to its independence from the British in 1947, that were codified in its Constitution, have created a country deeply committed to democracy.

Indians seem to value their democratic rights even more than they value order and stability. They were forced to choose between the two by Indira Gandhi, who declared a state of Emergency in the country in 1977, suspending democratic institutions on the grounds that forces within the country were creating disorder. For the next two years, strikes were prohibited and the trains in India ran on time. Slum dwellers were thrown out of cities and the cities began to be cleaned up. But when Indira Gandhi called an election in 1979, expecting that she would be elected for having restored order in the country, she was roundly defeated. Indians let it be known that their democracy was more precious to them than an imposed order.

Francis Fukuyama explains the history of China, the other huge Asian country with more than a billion people, in *The Origins of Political Order* (2011). China's history has been very different to India's. China's people have suffered from several long periods of political chaos along with painful disruptions of their economy and society. They have also experienced long periods of stability under emperors and dynasties that promulgated myths that they were descended from the heavens and that China was the centre of the earth. Fukuyama says that no Chinese government has accepted a rule of law. While the People's Republic of China has a written constitution, it is the Chinese Communist Party that is sovereign over the constitution. Similarly, in dynastic China, no emperor ever acknowledged the primacy of the legal source of authority; law was only the positive law that he himself made. He suggests that, in the absence of judicial checks on the power of the emperor, there was enormous scope for tyranny.

Confucius' rules of order specifying the roles and responsibilities of individuals within their families and society have influenced Chinese social values and systems of governance much more than Lao Tzu's contrarian philosophy urging individuals to be natural rather than conformers to social rules.

Influenced by different histories and different myths, the Chinese seem to value order and stability more than their personal freedoms than do Indians who set the balance differently.

THE TRINITY OF INSTITUTIONS

Government and business institutions have been recorded in the histories of China, India and other nations for thousands of years. Other forms of institutions, such as armies, have also been known for as long.

Civil society organizations (CSOs) are a recent category of institutions. The growth of CSOs, which include various forms of NGOs, is proving to be one of the strongest forces shaping the world in the last two decades. These organizations have many agendas and represent many causes. They come in many forms. With the advent of the Internet and mobile phones, many are virtual organizations that form across national boundaries with ease. They use a variety of means—generally peaceful but sometime violent—to convince (or shame) corporations and governments.

In fact, a reason for the emergence and growth of CSOs seems to be to shake up and change the established institutions of government and business. Not surprisingly, therefore, governments and businesses are now wishing to work in partnership with these organizations to improve societies. These three sets of institutions have become the trinity for change of the social order.

Institutional forms that pervade across societies, such as governments, businesses and CSOs (and armies), have cultures unique to themselves. Jane Jacobs, the social activist and author who popularized the concept of 'social capital', has analysed the differences in cultures of government organizations and business organizations.

In her book, *Systems of Survival* (1994) Jacobs has used a novel method for decoding the deeply embedded universal norms that drive behaviours in government and business organizations. Her book is an account of a didactic dialogue amongst six characters who explain and defend the ways in which governments and businesses must work. The group also includes a civil society activist who is critical of both business and government, as many civil society activists are!

Jacobs concludes that the symbiosis of two principal institutional forms—politics and government on one side, and commerce and business on the other—provides societies with the ability to progress and to govern themselves. Sustainable societies must have both. This is a warning to those extreme liberals and capitalists who would like governments to be banished, sometimes quoting Ronald Reagan who is reported to have said in some context, 'Government is not the solution; it is the problem.'

Jacobs describes politics and government as the 'guardian moral' syndrome of societies, and commerce and business as the 'commercial moral' syndrome. The contention between these two syndromes is very visible in India these days with many economic commentators suggesting that if India could just be rid of politicians and government the country would be much better off! However, the global financial crisis following the housing loan asset bubble in the US was a reminder that politicians and governments must provide societies with institutions that provide economies with stability and citizens with security.

The conclusion of Jacob's book is two lists of norms of behaviour that distinguish institutions with the guardian moral syndrome from those with the commercial moral syndrome. I list some of these norms here. For the rest, I recommend Jacob's book.

The guardian moral syndrome

- Shun trading
- Exert prowess

- Be obedient and disciplined
- Adhere to tradition
- Respect hierarchy
- Be loyal
- Dispense largesse

The commercial moral syndrome

- Shun force
- Come to voluntary agreements
- Collaborate easily with strangers and aliens
- Compete
- Use initiative and enterprise
- Be open to inventiveness and novelty
- Be efficient

Jacobs, a social activist herself, uses the character of the social activist in her book to tease out some of the undesirable behaviours of business and government organizations from a social activist's perspective. However, she does not analyse whether there are any universal codes of conduct of a 'civil society moral syndrome'.

Could there be some principles for shaping CSOs and their codes of conduct? This was a question examined in a remarkable conference in India in 1948, to which we will turn our attention in this chapter while we examine how India's history has shaped the three forms of institutions: business, government and civil society. We will also see how histories of nations can affect the shapes that universal forms of institutions, such as governments and business corporations, may take.

THE EVOLUTION OF BUSINESS, GOVERNMENT AND CIVIL SOCIETY INSTITUTIONS IN INDIA

The evolution of government, business and CSOs in India during the 19th and 20th centuries was influenced very strongly by two historical circumstances. One was the British rule of the country. The other was the non-violent movement for freedom of India from British rule.

First, consider how institutions of industry and business have been shaped. The growth of Indian industry was weakened by the British. British manufacturers used India as a source of raw materials, and also as a market for products manufactured in Britain—the typical relationship between European colonists and their colonies. Indian cotton went to mills in Manchester, and Indian jute to mills in Dundee. British merchants also used Indian spices, tea, indigo, and opium to expand their trade and businesses around the world.

Attempts by Indian pioneers to establish manufacturing industries were not encouraged, and were even thwarted. When Jamsetji Tata was determined to set up a steel mill in eastern India at the turn of the 19th century, using the abundant iron ore and coal in the region, he went to London to raise finance for his venture. Financiers there were persuaded by the British government to give him a cold reception. Tata had to return to India and appeal to the nationalist spirit of the Indians for funds. The result of the British attitude to Indian industry was that, at the time of India's independence in 1947, India had a very weak industrial sector for a country of its size and resources.

Let us turn now from industry to the state of CSOs in India at the time of Independence. India had built up a very large and strong civil society sector by 1947 because India obtained its freedom not by violent revolution but by the peaceful resistance of civil society and political organizations to British rule. These organizations mastered the art of peaceful mass mobilization. The methods they developed were later deployed by Martin Luther King in the civil resistance movement in the US, and by others in many countries.

The number of CSOs is growing rapidly all over the world and in India too. A study commissioned by the Indian government counted 3.3 million such entities in 2009. An increasing awareness of many problems, such as environmental degradation and abuse of human rights, that established institutions of government and business are failing to address adequately, has created a need for more CSOs. Indeed, some in civil society believe that businesses and governments may be the cause of these problems!

Changing values have contributed to the increased attention to environmental and societal issues. For example, awareness of the rights of children and women has undoubtedly increased all over the world in the past few decades. Accelerating the expanding awareness of problems is the increasing reach and speed of global communications, through satellite television and the Internet.

The case for voluntary CSOs was made by Acharya Vinoba Bhave in a remarkable meeting in Sevagram in central India in March 1948. The meeting had been convened by Mahatma Gandhi to discuss what type of institutions India would need to create an inclusive and just society. Among other things, he was concerned about the role of the Congress party which, having fought for India's independence from the British, could get corrupted as it began to govern the country. Unfortunately, he was assassinated on 30 January 1948 before that meeting. The discussions in this meeting, which was held after the Mahatma's death, have been recorded in a book, edited by his grandson, Gopalkrishna Gandhi, and Rupert Snell, *Gandhi is Gone, Who Will Guide Us Now?* (2007).

The fifty participants in this meeting included Jawaharlal

Nehru, Rajendra Prasad, Maulana Azad, Jayaprakash Narayan, Acharya Kripalani, Sucheta Kripalani, Zakir Hussain, Rajkumari Amrit Kaur, Vinoba Bhave, and Kamalnayan Bajaj. The need of the hour in March 1948 was for a strong government. The British had hastily divided the country and departed. With their exit, the edifice of government, and even the vaunted army in India that they had commanded, had to be divided into two, and all this amidst the holocaust created by the partition of India. Therefore, the creation of strong organizations to govern the country and assure security was uppermost in the minds of Nehru and many others. Other urgent problems, of having enough food to feed millions and enough jobs to provide them with incomes, also exercised the minds of the participants.

The question Gandhi had raised, about the role the Congress party would play in India's future, was also discussed. Should it be only a political party? Or should it be an organization for social work—a gigantic NGO, as it were? Should it have two wings—one for its political work and the other for its social work, and what would be the relationship between the two?

Mass movements for change, that rally people to stand up against or for something, require different organizational structures and processes for coordination of their activities than political parties would need to get organized to compete with other political parties. And governments, charged with running an administration, need organizational capabilities that political parties may not require. The different capabilities required for a movement, a political party, and then a government, became highlighted in India in 2012, when the Aam Admi Party (AAP), which had metamorphosed out of a mass campaign against corruption in 2011, did remarkably well in elections in the Delhi state and was unexpectedly called upon to form the government in December 2013. The government lasted less than fifty days.

At the meeting in Sevagram in March 1948, Vinoba Bhave made a case for a new form of organization unlike the hierarchical organizations necessary for government, political parties and large businesses. It would be a network of volunteers (and voluntary organizations). He explained that only such an organization could preserve the spirit of service to others, whereas hierarchical organizations would dissipate energies in internal matters and power politics. Acharya Kripalani supported Vinoba's argument. He is reported to have said: 'Without decentralization, democracy is an empty falsehood'. 'Centralization brings bureaucracy. Bureaucracy and technocracy are both equally the enemies of democracy. We shall tell Jawaharlal Nehru that if he is interested in real democracy, he will have to give up his craving for centralization (ibid.: 93).' Others in the meeting, while recognizing the need for a non-hierarchical form of organization, wondered how activities organized in the loose manner Vinoba Bhave proposed could ever be 'scaled up' to have a large effect. They discussed several ideas but could not find a satisfactory solution.

The challenge of finding ways to coordinate thousands, perhaps millions, of individual initiatives without excessive centralization that would kill their voluntary spirit confronts all business, government and political organizations when they expand. They centralize to coordinate expanding activities. But, in the process, they invariably smother the yearning in people for freedom to do their own thing, and to stand up for their own cause rather than do what they are told to do. Therefore, there is a need for other forms of organization in which people can coordinate with other like-minded collaborators without any bosses to make them work together, and in which they serve because they care for the cause rather than the financial compensation and hierarchical authority that conventional organizations offer as rewards for good work. These are 21st century questions of institutional design that have become universal.

Gandhi, a great innovator of institutions, who upheld the norm of non-violence in all matters, including resistance against violence, and had developed forms of organization and action to apply this norm in practice, had noted that the character of the Congress must change, from an organization to mobilize for India's independence to an organization for effective self-governance, with the change in context that would come about with India's independence.

Let us now turn to the third set of Indian institutions—government—and the influence of the British on them. The conference in Sevagram in 1948, on a new role and form for the Congress party, could not achieve consensus because Jawaharlal Nehru, India's first prime minister, had great need to ensure law and order in the country, which had broken down with the partition of the country and the ensuing riots along religious lines. Also, the government had to provide shelter and housing to millions of refugees. The country needed strong government organizations and had to turn to those left behind by the British: the army, police and civil services. The British had designed these organizations to serve their purposes of controlling India, and they served the new Indian government very well at its time of need.

The civil service set up by the British in India, the Indian Civil Service (ICS), has been described as the 'iron frame' that kept the country together. Young officers were trained to use authority to maintain law and order, with the assistance of the police, in the large districts assigned to them, and to collect revenues for the government. With Independence, the developmental Indian state set itself new goals. Education and health care for the masses that had been neglected by the British had to be improved. Private enterprises had to be encouraged and assisted to grow to create employment and also to reduce India's dependence on imports.

Command-and-control institutions, like the ICS and its successor, the Indian Administrative Service (IAS), organized on the same lines, were not equipped for the fundamentally different roles they were now expected to perform. To this day, the principles guiding their conduct and their relationship with citizens have not changed sufficiently from the command-and-control mentality of their heritage to enable them to perform new developmental roles effectively.

The internal management structures of these institutions are hierarchical. People lower down in these vertical hierarchies look upward to their superiors for instruction. Such vertical obedience is necessary for good command-and-control organizations. Secrecy and aloofness from the public are codes of conduct required in command-and-control organizations; transparency in their internal activities and decisions, which would build citizens' trust, is not a norm these organizations can easily adopt.

The 'vertical' orientation of these organizations results in a plethora of organizational 'silos' when the scope of government expands to cover more developmental areas, as has happened in India. Ministries and departments proliferate but they do not coordinate laterally. This has become a big handicap for the government to perform its role in development. In development programmes, many organizations must work together to achieve the outcomes the country needs. For example, the problem of stunted growth of India's children compared to other countries—described as the chronic problem of 'child malnutrition' in India—can only be addressed holistically by improving sanitation, clean drinking water, maternal health and education of mothers, as well as providing balanced diets. This requires collaboration amongst many ministries and departments of government. To achieve this, government organizations must change their orientations to work laterally with their peers rather than vertically for their superiors.

India's principal political party, the Indian National Congress (INC), which was in the vanguard of the freedom movement, and for whose redesign Gandhi had called the meeting in Sevagram in 1948, has become less democratic and more centralized since then. Its centralization was accelerated by Indira Gandhi. And with her ascent to power, the party was set towards becoming a dynasty. Following her, her son, Rajiv Gandhi, became prime minister. Then her daughter-in-law, Sonia Gandhi, became the president of the Congress party. Sonia Gandhi chose not to become prime minister when she led the party to a stunning victory in the national elections in 2004. Instead, she anointed a loyal technocrat, Dr Manmohan Singh, as the prime minister, while she has called the shots on all important appointments and policies. Now her son, Rahul Gandhi, is being called upon to do his dynastic duty and lead the Congress party. Unfortunately, many other Indian political parties have also adopted similar autocratic and dynastic structures.

More than sixty years after its independence, India's governance structures retain elements of the British government of India: civil services designed like iron frames (though rusting rapidly) and monarchical political parties in place of the British monarchy.

Over these years, the world has been changing and India too. The forces of change in the world and in India have been explained earlier. The inability of India's institutions of governance to change adequately has resulted in the growing decline of citizens' trust in them. Reform of institutions has become imperative.

CHANGING INSTITUTIONS

Behaviours of institutions and organizations cannot be changed merely by changing the written rules—the laws and manuals of procedure. Written rules cannot easily overrule more deeply embedded unwritten rules which are the norms and traditions of societies and institutions that have evolved with their histories.

To change the behaviour of an organization one must understand what causes it to behave as it does. For this, both its written as well as its unwritten rules must be understood. The written rules the organization is supposed to be following could be mapped by examining all the laws and rules and procedures that have been prescribed. These are only the 'espoused theories', not the '*actual* theories-in-use' guiding the organization's behaviour. To understand the actual theories-in-use—which are the combinations of the written and unwritten rules—that induce people to do what they do in a society or an organization, one must enquire more deeply into the drivers of their behaviour.

During the 1990s, I attended several annual meetings of the international Society of Organizational Learning (SOL) in the Mount Washington Hotel in Bretton Woods, New Hampshire. In 1944, delegates from forty-four nations had gathered in the same hotel to design institutions for the post-war recovery of the global economy. The General Agreement on Tariffs and Trade (GATT) was signed here and agreements were executed to establish the International Bank for Reconstruction and Development (the World Bank) and the International Monetary Fund (IMF).

SOL was a very large gathering of hundreds of consultants and academics, meeting half a century later in the Mount Washington Hotel, searching for ways to change the world that the historic conference of 1944 had helped to create. The world had experienced unprecedented material progress in the intervening fifty years. These evangelists—and so many were—wanted to correct some of the side effects of materialist progress—the destruction of the environment, the fragmentation of communities, and the loss of meaning in personal lives. But they were practical persons, mostly. They would compare the methods they had developed to bring about change in organizations and institutions. Case studies were presented. Techniques and toolkits were advertised.

SOL was a marketplace for methods to make change happen. In many ways, it anticipated changes in the study of economics. Economics today is drifting from its limited view of a rational, self-interested and utility maximizing humans being towards a more holistic understanding of human beings. Emotions influence human actions. The mind is not simply a rational calculator. The human mind understands the world and takes decisions in ways that economists have yet to comprehend. What motivates human beings, and how human beings relate to and make sense of their environments, were questions that engaged the consultants and academics at SOL.

My profession at the time was to help people in organizations to learn to work more effectively together so that they could produce the change they would all benefit from. It was called 'organization transformation' or 'change management'. From the large pool of knowledge of SOL's practitioners, and my own extensive reading and experience, I have learned three truths about institutional transformation:

1. People's 'theories-in-use' about how things are done and should be done are difficult to change. Such theories arise from the histories of societies, as well as individuals' own histories. They are rules of behaviour that people have learned for success in their environments. People cannot give up these theories easily. These are the guide-rails that they instinctively rely on.
2. The only condition under which people may give up a 'theory-in-use', and be willing to try another, is if an even stronger and deeper force urges them to do so. That deeper force can be a 'crisis of aspiration'. When people consciously connect with their deepest unfulfilled aspirations they may realize that what is preventing them from reaching their goals is the

holding on to an inappropriate theory-in-use for its realization. Then they may be willing to let go of one set of guide-rails to reach out for another. This insight led to the discovery of an important step in designing processes of transformational change in organizations. This step is to make people connect with their deep aspirations before they examine the difficulties they encounter.

3. Organizations do not exist in a vacuum. They are parts of much larger systems composed of other organizations around them, as well as wider forces that impact all of them. An understanding is necessary of what these forces are that can enable or disable attempts of an organization and its members to change and obtain what they aspire for. The process of scenario planning, which has been introduced in the previous chapter, provides a way to understand these forces around the organization.

American theologian Reinhold Niebuhr said: 'God grant me the serenity to accept the things I cannot change, the courage to change the things I can, and the wisdom to know the difference.' The acceptance that we are parts of a larger system is wisdom. Acceptance of circumstances with serenity is considered to be an Eastern trait, associated with Eastern religious and spiritual traditions, especially Buddhism and Hinduism. In contrast, in Western scientific traditions, Man seeks the power to change anything in the world. According to the scientific culture that flowed out of the Enlightenment in Europe in the 18th century, he only has to discover how.

The implications of these two ways of perceiving the relationship of Man with the world around him, especially the natural world, has profound implications for the survival of ecosystems. In one view, Nature is there for Man to use and to change for his own goals. In the other view, Man is a part of the natural world and is shaped by it. These contrasting views also translate into different approaches to changing institutions and organizations, to which we turn in the next chapter.

4

REDESIGNING THE AEROPLANE WHILE FLYING

There is nothing more difficult to take in hand, more perilous to conduct or more uncertain in its success, than to take a lead in the introduction of a new order of things.

—NICCOLO DI BERNANDO MACHIAVELLI

Resistance to change, especially radical change, is a typical reaction. The general response to any new theory or new idea is resistance. One tends to dwell on all manners of problems, real or otherwise, that might render the theory invalid. But then history abounds with examples of things considered impossible or stupid that have not only come to pass, but are hailed as wonderful ideas. Those who recognize the merits of these ideas at the right point of time reap immense benefits and those who don't fall far behind.

In the world of ideas and paradigms, there is always a transition period during which the emergence of a fundamental change is not recognized. People tend to seek solutions for new situations in the old framework. It takes them, at least most of them, a long time to devise and accept the innovations that can meet the requirements of the new situation. The inability or unwillingness to question currently accepted principles underlies many of the problems organizations and societies have in changing when necessary.

A challenge to prevailing beliefs about how things really work is disconcerting for many and irrelevant for others. When Copernicus first pointed out that the earth revolved around the sun, the reactions of the Church and 'scientists' of the time were so strong that his theory had to be published with the disclaimer that it had no claim to be fact, but was only one man's idea! For farmers at the time (and perhaps even most people today) Copernicus' theory did not make much difference. For them it was sufficient to observe that the sun somehow rises and sets. But for navigators it is necessary to know the real pattern of planetary motions. So, too, some organizations and societies may continue to operate with old principles, but for those who aspire to thrive amidst rapid and unpredictable change, it is time to question old principles of leadership and organization.

Three sets of ideas are explored in this chapter. The first is a framework to explain different types of learning, ranging from learning about simple procedures and routines to learning new theories. It is especially difficult for very successful societies, companies and people to give up theories that have brought them exceptional success. Their 'special way' of doing things is greatly admired. It becomes wrapped up with their identity. Success brings laurels. Then people rest on these laurels. The risk to them is that they may rust on their laurels while the world around them changes. We need to create institutions that are not lost in 'the dreary desert sand of dead habit', in the words of Rabindranath Tagore.

The second set of ideas in this chapter is insights from the ways in which 'complex self-adaptive systems', such as systems in nature, maintain their ability to evolve when their environment changes. What can we learn from these systems to guide the design of human institutions and organizations that will maintain their abilities to change even while they are successfully performing?

How can we redesign our planes while we are successfully flying in them?

The third related set of ideas is concepts of leadership required for learning societies and organizations.

THE LEARNING FIELD

Change-makers have to lead organizations and, at the same time, they have to themselves learn new concepts and skills of leading.

We can break this challenge along two dimensions. The first is *who* is learning? As mentioned already, the leader herself has to learn. But the leader has to also enable a group or an organization to learn. The need for new learning may even extend beyond a single organization to several organizations that have to interact. It could also extend to a larger community, as in the case of the leader who wishes to improve the way a city functions.

The other dimension is *what* the nature of learning should be. For our purposes we can distinguish four levels of learning. The first, the Know-What level, is the level at which new information and new procedural routines are learned. Most so-called 'knowledge management' systems that are designed to store and provide access to information to those who may need it lead to learning at this level. Many training programmes that teach new procedures, such as procedures for using a computer effectively, also focus on learning at this level.

The next higher level of learning, the Know-How level, deals with learning about the architecture of processes and about distinguishing categories of knowledge. To use a simple example, the process of cooking involves many procedures such as turning on the stove, peeling a potato, etc. However, knowledge of any or all of these procedures does not by itself make a great cook. Good cooks know how to combine these procedures in a process that produces a great dish. In fact, many great cooks delegate almost all the routine procedures to assistants while they orchestrate the whole process. Thus they have the know-how that is over and above the knowledge of individual procedures.

The third and still higher level, the Know-Why level, is knowledge of the theory of the subject: which is an understanding of the reason *why* things happen. Nowadays, everyone acknowledges the role science has played in the development of new technologies. Science explains the 'why', from which flows technology that provides the 'how' to make things happen. Thus, an understanding of the 'why' enables the crafting of more effective processes. Clearly there is great leverage in understanding 'why', even though practical managers are often uncomfortable with discussing concepts and theories. They want to move from 'theoretical' speculation to 'practical' stuff. They seem to forget that there is nothing as practical as a good theory because of what it can enable a manager to do!

Our ingrained mental models or theories become hindrances when we want to achieve a result that we are unable to obtain with the approaches we are used to. And overcoming these hindrances is very difficult. First, since mental models by their very definition are tacit and not explicit—in other words they are in the back of our heads where we cannot see them and not in front of our eyes where we can examine them—they are extremely slippery to handle. And, second, since they have worked for us so far, it becomes very difficult to perceive them as obstacles. Why give up something which has proven its worth over and over again?

Only the strongest type of inner motivation can catalyse us into letting go of ingrained theory and finding new theories. It is only when we realise that our mental models are preventing us from obtaining something that we dearly care about can we abandon them. If the 'want' is not stronger than the discomfort of 'letting go', we will not make room in our minds for learning a new theory to replace the old. Therefore, the greatest leverage for new learning is in recognizing the deepest wants that are not fulfilled, and accepting that the theory and approach currently in use cannot fulfil this want.

Therefore, the fourth and the highest is the level of Know-Want. But what has wanting and caring for something got to do with learning, some may ask? Surely learning is about cognition and rationalization. However, as Howard Gardner has explained in his 1983 book, *Frames of Mind: The Theory of Multiple Intelligences*, human beings operate with multiple intelligences, including logical, bodily and interpersonal intelligences. In fact, techniques of working with 'emotional intelligence' are now creeping into mainstream management since Daniel Goleman wrote his bestselling book, *Emotional Intelligence: Why it can matter more than IQ* in 1995.

This must happen. Because most of the processes we use in life are not technological processes derived from the physical sciences. They are also social and emotional processes. For example, the process for interacting with other people is something we use all the time. It is based on some mental model, or theory, at the back of our heads, of why some behaviours are more appropriate than others. Similarly, we use many management and leadership processes in our lives and these are all based on some underlying mental models. People who use different approaches to management generally have different mental models or theories of effectiveness. These models or theories, while often not articulated, are well ingrained. And when people are successful in what they do, they have no need to question their underlying mental models.

By putting the two dimensions of learning together, on one side who is learning and on the other the levels of learning, we can describe a 'Learning Field' (Figure 4.1). The Learning Field is useful to understand what the learning agenda needs to be to produce the required change.

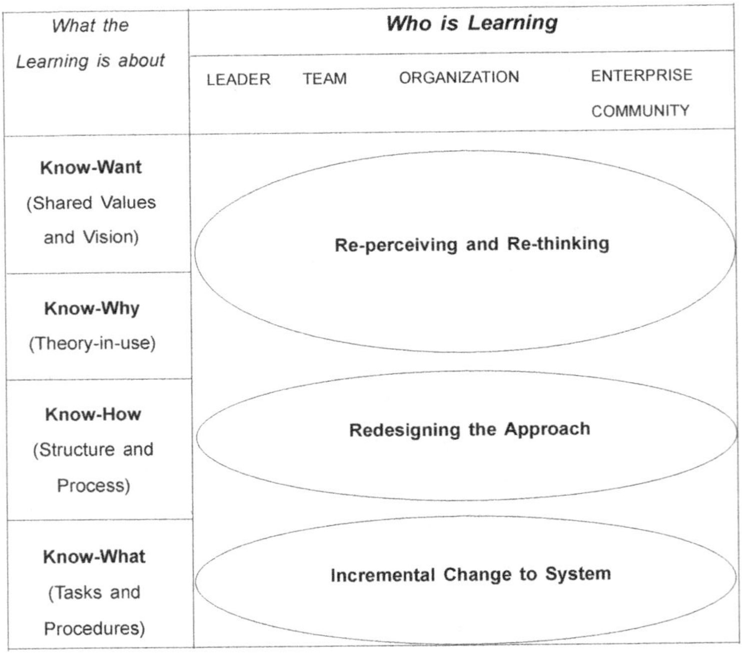

What the Learning is about	Who is Learning			
	LEADER	TEAM	ORGANIZATION	ENTERPRISE COMMUNITY
Know-Want (Shared Values and Vision)	Re-perceiving and Re-thinking			
Know-Why (Theory-in-use)	^			
Know-How (Structure and Process)	Redesigning the Approach			
Know-What (Tasks and Procedures)	Incremental Change to System			

Figure 4.1: Learning Field

The model of the learning field suggests that for mobilizing change in a community's approach to its shared surroundings it may be necessary to develop a shared aspirational vision of the environment that the community would like to create. In other words, to start at the Know-Want level. Once the aspiration is created, the community would then move on to the Know-Why stage. It can be motivated to examine just why it cannot realize this want with its present model of governance.

Thereafter, the design of new governance and management processes, the Know-How, can follow from the new model of community governance that is adopted. And the Know-What, the new procedures that are required by the new processes, would flow accordingly.

Now let us look at the horizontal dimension of the Learning Field. When change-makers want to lead others, especially those who would not accept their authority blindly, they have to enable the group, organization or community, to want to do something together. Then they have to enable people to develop a shared mental model—a collective Know-Why, especially if a fundamental change in approach is required to get an organization or community 'unstuck'. Leadership is a process of enabling people to want to move together, and to be able to do so effectively. Types and sizes of organizations may vary, but the underlying principles are the same.

Mahatma Gandhi demonstrated the power of a shared Know-Want and the adoption of a radically new theory of how to obtain it as he galvanized India in the first half of the last century. Non-violence was a very novel approach to fight for the freedom that Indians wanted.

COMPLEX SELF-ADAPTIVE SYSTEMS

When the Soviet Union collapsed towards the end of the last century, American political scientist Francis Fukuyama famously described it as the 'end of history'. His thesis was that several ideological battles that had raged through the 20th century had come to an end. Amongst the battles that the United States (US) (and its loyal ally, the United Kingdom) seemed to have won against the Soviet Union was about the role of government in the economy. In the Soviet system, government controlled the economy through minute planning and allocations of resources—a system that

India's Planning Commission had also adopted. Ronald Reagan and Margaret Thatcher fought off encroachments of government in their countries' economies even as they fought off the Soviet Union militarily. Alan Greenspan, chairman of the US Federal Reserve in the 1990s, went further to let the financial sector free of regulations. The consequence of these swings too far against government and regulation was the global financial crash within the first decade of the 21st century.

Now it is safe to say that neither 'leave it to the market', nor top-down planning and control is the solution. A third solution is required to govern economies. Insights into systems' architecture can provide governments new concepts for managing complex financial and industrial systems.

Broadly, complex systems may be divided into three classes. One is 'engineered' systems. These are systems designed by man, following scientific disciplines, to produce desired outcomes. Machines are the most common manifestation of this class of systems. So are top-down planning systems that control inputs and outputs. However, as all students of engineering must learn, engineered systems are subject to the Second Law of Dynamics. This law says that the entropy within a system (roughly translatable as confusion within) will inevitably increase over time. Therefore, the capability of an engineered system will reduce over time. The operation of the law is evident in our experience. Machines must be periodically repaired and renovated by engineers to maintain their levels of performance. And we also know from experience that while planned economies may start vigorously, they lose their abilities over time. Moreover, physical scientists can explain, with mathematical models, that an increase in entropy is inevitable in engineered systems.

The second class of systems is 'chaotic' systems. These are formed by the interactions of millions of independent particles or free agents. The concept of a universally free market composed of free agents without any governmental regulation, that liberal market extremists espouse, has the structure of a chaotic system. Chaotic systems can produce surprising outcomes. The example of a butterfly flapping its wings in Brazil that causes storms in Hong Kong is often cited to illustrate this characteristic of chaotic systems. The near collapse of the global financial system, stemming from problems in the housing loan market in the US, could be another example. Mathematicians and physical scientists are studying the mechanisms by which the consequences of local events transmit across large systems to understand the structures of chaotic systems.

The third class of systems is complex 'self-adaptive' systems. Insights into these have come from a collaborative, interdisciplinary exploration of systems by economists, physical scientists, evolutionary biologists, computer systems experts and others interested in the behaviour of complex systems. One of the best known of these interdisciplinary forums is the Santa Fe Institute. It was founded in 1984 in Santa Fe, USA, by Nobel laureates in economics and the physical sciences and eminent theoretical biologists and computer scientists.

Complex self-adaptive systems display characteristics that neither engineered systems nor chaotic systems have. They increase their capabilities over time unlike engineered systems, and they do this with some underlying logic unlike random chaotic systems. The most obvious illustrations of such systems are in nature where capabilities of species evolve through competition. Thus, over time, more evolved species develop. Contrary to the Second Law of Thermodynamics, natural systems follow a law of evolutionary biology that says that complex systems will increase their capability over time. The competition in nature does not destroy the whole system. There is some higher order, or some deeper structures—depending on whether one believes in God or is an atheist—that regulates this competition so that the 'commons' on which all depend are maintained. It is on these commons that the competitive game plays out, evolving better capabilities in the system over time.

They sit 'on the edge' between engineered systems and chaotic systems. They neither sink into stasis like engineered systems nor are they an unformed, potentially chaotic mass. They have an underlying architecture that gives them the capability to evolve from a lesser order to a higher order. Policymakers and institutional designers need a new theory to govern the dynamics of national and international economies and societies. They shun planning and controls. And they no longer want an unregulated economy and society. They would be well guided by emerging insights into the architecture of complex self-adaptive systems.

ARCHITECTURAL PRINCIPLES

What can we learn from the emerging research into complex self-adaptive systems, such as biological systems, that would apply to the design of human institutions and organizations? To answer this question, a framework that describes the essential elements of an organized human system is necessary. We need this filter or lens through which we can select what is applicable from the fascinating material that is becoming available on complex self-adaptive systems. Without the filter, one could pick up a bunch of curious and romantic ideas that may not be applicable to human institutions. At the same time, the filter must be broad enough so that it does not screen out any unusual idea merely because it does not fit the detailed mental model of the filter designer about what is relevant to business and social organizations.

An organized human system (a definition that covers business entities, government organizations, and non-governmental organizations or NGOs) consists of four fundamental components. First, all such systems use 'resources' of many types, and these include people, technologies, machines, etc. The composition of resources varies with the nature of the entity. Second, these resources are 'organized' in some manner. Third, the resources in the organization are deployed in 'processes' to produce results. Last but not least, all of this—the processes, organization and resources—are sought to be 'directed' towards the goals of the entity. So, goals and direction, organization, processes, and resources are the four fundamental components.

These four seem to be the minimum set of components required to describe a social or business system. Take any one of them away and the description seems incomplete. More can be added but they would most likely be an expansion of one of these four basic building blocks.

The study of complex self-adaptive systems reveals one critical principle for each of the four components of a complex human system thereby making a minimal critical set of principles. The four components and four principles are described in Figure 4.2.

Aligned Aspiration

Human systems differ from all other, non-human, complex systems with regard to the process of choosing goals and setting a direction. Human beings have the ability, and the urge, to consciously project themselves into the future. They can visualize futures they want to create and live in, whereas other complex systems, such as ecological systems, do not have this ability as far as we know. Perhaps these systems are also evolving towards some goal. But it is not clear whether the components of the system—the flora and fauna and the rest—have chosen the goal! Hence, there may not be much to be learned from complex self-adaptive systems which are not human that may be relevant to the process by which human systems imagine their futures and set their goals.

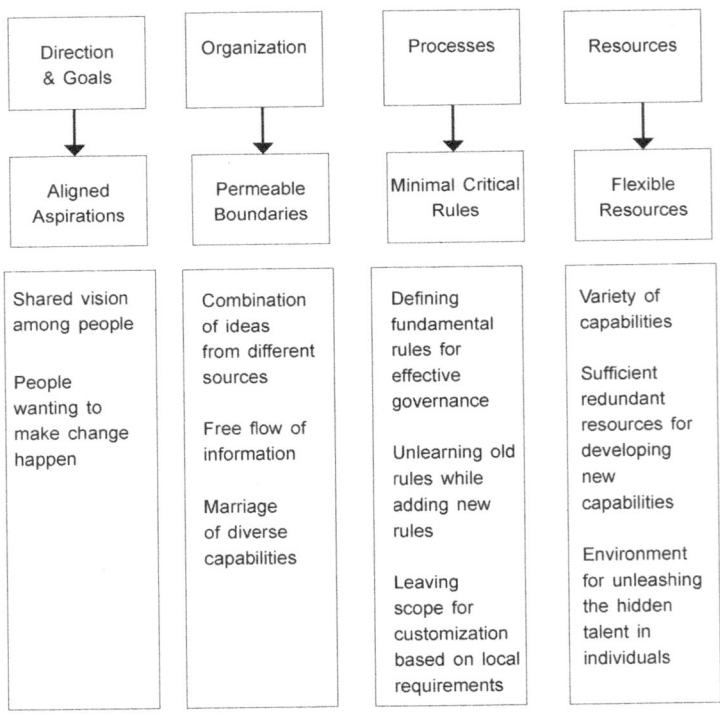

Figure 4.2: Principles of Complex Self-Adaptive Systems

The principle that applies to the setting of direction in human organizations, ranging from business organizations and NGOs to nations, is 'Aligned Aspirations'. Both words are important. The goal has to be aspirational. It must be something people really care about, and really want. Otherwise they will not be inspired to stretch themselves to create that future. And there has to be a conscious alignment of aspirations and goals to bring together the force of many intelligences that can make seemingly impossible things possible.

Permeable Boundaries

Let us now look at the other three components of complex self-adaptive systems. Let me introduce the principles that apply to these components by analysing a complex self-adaptive system that is very modern and very 'techie' and then support these principles by insights from natural systems. Let us consider the evolution of the Internet. The Internet is a very complex system in many ways. It connects many subsystems all over the world, each of which works to its own rules. People are putting in and taking out things from the Internet all the time. It is also a very adaptive system—it enables functions that people have not conceived before. In addition, innovations continue to be found.

The power of the Internet comes from its ability to enable 'end-to-end' connections. Switch on. Write a message to anyone anywhere. Put the address. Click. And off it goes across boundaries of organizations and countries. It is widely acknowledged that the Internet has stimulated many innovations and social change by bringing a huge variety of ideas and people together very quickly and easily. There does not seem to be any significant field of human endeavour that has not been touched already by the Internet's innovative environment, be it business, education, research, government or entertainment.

Some people do not like so much freedom. They have political reasons, cultural reasons, economic reasons, or technical reasons to wish to curtail this complete freedom, which they fear can lead to chaos.

People in power rightly fear the consequences of this free flow of information and opinions to their constituents from all sorts of sources from the Internet. Hence they try, sometimes, like King Canute, to roll back the waves that may wash them away.

Parents fear that their children may see and hear things, as they surf the Internet, that are not good for them to learn. Sometimes it is not the parents but others who are outraged that children in general should have access to such ideas.

Napster stretched, beyond the limit perhaps, some current foundational principles of economics. By enabling Internet users to download music for free, it violated the rights of the owners of intellectual property to obtain financial rewards for their creativity and investments.

At the same time, the rapid growth of the Internet and 'social media' (which the Internet has enabled) is creating political and technical problems which some suggest can only be resolved by curbing the freedom of people to communicate freely, 'end-to-end'.

The founders of the Internet, who have separately contributed to its creation, are worried, according to *The Economist* (2001). Vint Cerf, Steve Deering, Tim Berners-Lee, and also Ray Ozzie (the man behind Lotus Notes) have expressed their fear that such fixes will destroy a basic principle of the Internet, which is 'permeable boundaries', so that there can be 'end-to-end' communication. This principle creates the Internet's uniquely vibrant ecosystem, in which innovation flourishes and unexpected new applications spring up overnight.

A lesson one can draw from the evolution of the Internet and its present problems is the critical principle that applies to 'Organization', the second component of complex human systems. This principle is 'permeable boundaries'. Permeability of boundaries enables the combination of ideas, which can produce innovative solutions, and also prevent ossification of systems behind their walls.

In nature, too, the water's edge, where land and water mingle, is always the most fecund source of new forms of life, whereas the impervious boundaries of rock faces are not. In nature also crossbreeding is the source of healthy evolution, whereas inbreeding results in regression over time.

There seems to be an inexorable tendency in organizations, in governments and in businesses to create internal walls when they seek order and pursue efficiency. They create these walls by creating specialized roles, narrowing performance evaluations, and even by incentive systems that reward individual contributions. All these measures—specialization, precise performance evaluations and incentives linked directly to individual and departmental performance—seem logical for managing an organization in a disciplined manner. But they very often result in reducing internal collaboration and creating internal silos. Therefore, leaders must continue to test whether there is permeability in the organization's boundaries. And they must prevent the walls from rising by instituting appropriate practices.

Minimal Critical Rules

Let us now look at the third of the four components of organized, complex human systems, viz. Processes. Let us get into this by asking the question, 'What holds the Internet together?' The answer is: a set of simple rules or protocols.

The Internet and the World Wide Web have enabled people everywhere to communicate with each other, and to send, search and store very complicated information on almost anything under the sun. The creation of this huge and unprecedented knowledge sharing capability did not require the development of any new computers, nor the laying down of any dedicated telecommunication systems. It 'happened' because standards were adopted for a few essential procedures.

Tim Berners-Lee, the inventor of the World Wide Web, has

been hailed by *Time* as one of the greatest minds of the 20th century. In his book, *Weaving the Web* (2000: 36), Berners-Lee describes how the Web came about:

> The art was to define the few basic rules, common rules of "protocol" that would allow one computer to talk to another, in such a way that when all computers everywhere did it, the system would thrive, not break down. For the Web, those elements were, in decreasing order of importance, Universal Resource Identifiers (URIs), the Hypertext Transfer Protocol (HTTP), and the Hypertext Markup Language (HTML).

And, Berners-Lee adds,

> What was often difficult for people to understand about the design was that there was nothing else beyond URIs, HTTP, and HTML. There was no central computer "controlling" the Web, no single protocol on which these protocols worked, not even an organisation anywhere that "ran" the Web.

Somehow we have a mental model that anything huge, involving lots of people and lots of activity, must require a lot of effort to control it. We also believe that complex situations require complex solutions. While the truth is that complex situations are best resolved by very simple solutions and governed by very few rules.

In the early 1980s, the Western world was overtaken by the prowess of Japanese companies to produce products of a quality that Western firms could not match, and at costs that the Western firms considered unattainable. What is more, Japanese firms swamped the markets with continuing streams of new models of consumer electronic gadgets, cars, watches, and many other products. Their Western competitors could not understand how the

Japanese could do this. To the Western mind then, the management of such complexity in manufacturing would require the mastery of complex coordination algorithms and huge computer capabilities.

In the early 1980s, some Japanese companies began to invite executives from other countries to study their operations. I was a member of one such delegation that toured leading Japanese companies to discover what was at the heart of their management prowess. We met Prof Ishikawa, who along with Prof Deming is considered to be the father of the Total Quality Movement (TQM) in Japan. We visited many companies, but the visit that made the greatest impression on me was to Toyota. Toyota is credited by Japanese companies to have developed the production system that enabled Japanese companies to perform the miracle that Western managers did not understand at the time. Toyota, and its novel production system, has been rightly described as 'the machine that changed the world' by an MIT study of the automobile industry worldwide.

So here we were in Toyota's headquarters in Nagoya, listening to their chief of industrial engineering describe the Toyota production system. It was so simple! One simple rule: do not produce anything till it is wanted. In other words, do not produce in anticipation of demand. And there was a simple 'kanban' (or bin card) that moved from machine to machine and assembler to supplier when it was time to produce the next part. No computers. No central production control hierarchy.

A manager of a European auto company was incredulous. He knew that a multi-product car factory was a very complex system. After all, he ran one. Such a factory has thousands of machines and thousands of people, producing and assembling thousands of different parts. So did Toyota's factory. We knew this because we had just visited it. We had been amazed to see that there was hardly any inventory of parts between machines and assembly stations, in spite of the variety of models produced. High variety, unmatched quality, low costs and low inventories, what an unbeatable combination!

That is why Toyota was beating his company, the European manager realized. And this Japanese guy was saying they used only simple rules and simple forms! The European turned to us and said in exasperation, 'The Japanese never tell you their real secrets, do they!' He could not understand that something complex could be managed with simple rules. He would find it even harder to believe that Toyota was performing far better than his company because it followed simple rules.

Chris Langton of the Santa Fe Institute has experimented with Game of Life, a computer program that produces evolving 'life-like' patterns. A few simple rules enable the program to create very orderly patterns. When he would add a few more good rules to improve the patterns and to speed up the process, the system did not seem to respond well. If he added a few more rules to correct the side effects of the previous rules, the system would start to go into disorder. This intrigued Langton. All the rules were good rules. Each was added to take care of a problem that had been noticed. Then why did the system's performance deteriorate as more good rules were added? he wondered. It struck him that the number of rules also has an effect on the system's capability to change and evolve gracefully, not merely the goodness of the rules.

Stuart Kaufmann and John Holland, also with the Santa Fe Institute, have confirmed this. They experimented with computer programs that learn new and better rules to make themselves more effective. Holland developed the notion of an 'economy of rules'. Which means that while a system needs rules to run itself, it needs only a minimal set of critical rules. Adding more rules, even good rules in themselves, causes disorder in the system.

The lesson, therefore, is this: while 'learning organizations' will learn new rules, they must remember the principle of Minimal Critical Rules, and shed ('unlearn') some rule as they add another good rule. Unfortunately, organizations are quick to add rules, and are not at all systematic in shedding rules.

Flexible Pool of Resources

The fourth component in our framework of a complex human system is Resources. Companies, communities and countries, all use resources to produce the value they need. The resources include physical resources and they also include the knowledge and talents of people. Organizations that wish to evolve to higher order capabilities must have flexibility in their resource pool. There are three ways in which organizations can ensure that they have the required flexibility in the resources available to them. One is by 'requisite variety' in the resources. The second is through 'adequate redundancy'. A third way of obtaining flexibility is through the 'latent potential' in the resources.

Stephen Jay Gould, an authority on evolutionary biology, explains how these principles work in biological species, thereby enabling them to evolve. The principle of 'requisite variety' is simplest to understand. Systems that do not have requisite variety run the danger of losing their vitality as a result of inbreeding. Hence it is necessary to ensure that the gene pool is rich and sufficiently varied.

The Internet has enabled innovation by bringing together a variety of people and ideas that could not have got together so easily earlier. One of the reasons why the US is a source of many innovations in many fields is said to be the variety of people that come together in the US 'melting pot'. It is worth noting that in the US, immigrants are not restricted to the lower level, labour-intensive jobs. Immigrants to the country are also to be found in senior positions in corporations, academia and research, where they participate in shaping new ideas and policies.

What this implies is that countries and companies that shut out outsiders from their knowledge creating pools run the risk of stagnation. They may be very efficient while they lead in a game they have mastered. But when the game changes, they are unable to innovate and change. Could this be one of the reasons, one wonders, why Japan is now stagnating after it dominated the world earlier with its prowess in efficient operations? Inbreeding has certainly been found to be a problem in many companies across the world that had earlier developed strong and unique cultures by always promoting from within. Many such companies have now opened themselves to lateral hiring at very senior levels to inject some fresh thinking into their strategies.

'Adequate redundancy' may be the idea which efficiency-oriented managers will have most difficulty with. But let us see why it is important. Consider the human body as an example. It is a very efficient machine. The chemical, physical and cognitive processes it can perform are amazing. These abilities are related to the genes in the body. We have now begun to understand how these genes work and what each of them does. Let us suppose that every gene was required for a function of the human body and mind. In other words, a perfectly engineered or 're-engineered' machine with all unnecessary genes removed. Now suppose the body needed to adapt itself to a new capability. Which gene could it spare to experiment and learn this capability? It could not afford to let any of its genes 'off the hook' because that would affect the body's ongoing functions. Hence the evolution of new capabilities would be severely hampered, if not impossible.

The third way in which biological species have the capabilities in their resources to evolve is through the 'latent potential' in their resources. Gould gives the example of how birds developed wings to fly. Feathers are an essential component of a bird's flying apparatus.

But birds did not originally develop feathers so that they could fly. Feathers were first developed for their thermal capabilities, to keep the bodies of birds warm. Later, the 'latent potential' of feathers as flying apparatus was taken advantage of, when birds needed to fly to find food and to escape from predators.

Imagine a 'value engineer' examining a bird before birds had learned to fly. He would redesign the feathers to improve their thermal efficiency, or even replace them with something else that is more effective for keeping the bird warm. Thus he would unwittingly strip the feathers of their potential as flying apparatus thereby creating a very warm species of bird perhaps, but one that may soon die of hunger, or be gobbled up by a predator. A 'value engineer', looking with a clinical eye at all parts of an organization, seeks to strip out the capabilities whose contribution to the performance of the system is not clear. Thus latent capabilities that could be the source of valuable innovations can be thrown aside.

We now have four principles, one for each of the four basic components of a complex human system. Let us recapitulate them.

Direction and Goals	:	Aligned Aspiration
Organization	:	Permeable Boundaries
Processes	:	Minimal Critical Rules
Resources	:	Flexibility in Pool

Thus we have four basic components and one fundamental principle for each, adding up to a minimum critical set of principles for human institutions that can learn, adapt and grow.

NEW MODELS OF LEADERSHIP

Musical metaphors are often used to describe leadership and organizations. A very commonly used metaphor of a leader is the conductor of a symphony orchestra. Conductors produce orderly music from the combination of many different talents and resources. The problem with this metaphor is that the symphony orchestra plays a set, pre-written piece of music. The pre-written score is like the overall plan in a centrally managed economy, which specifies what every person must do. The conductor-leader ensures they all know what they are supposed to do and how. The individual players do not have much flexibility to innovate.

In the last few years, another metaphor for organizations and leadership has appeared, that of the jazz combo. Jazz combos allow individual players greater freedom to innovate. Every time the combo plays the same number it can be quite different. The combo can respond to the mood of the audience. This seems a better metaphor for organizations today that have to be nimble and responsive to customer needs, while also giving room to individuals within them to be creative. The structures that enable the combo players to coordinate with each other, while they experiment with variations, are the melody and the rhythm, rather than a detailed score.

Let us lay the different types of structures for producing alignment used by these two different forms of musical ensembles onto the framework of the Learning Field that we explained earlier. Symphony orchestras provide detailed instructions at the Know-What level: which note to play when. On the other hand, jazz combos provide an architecture or model of the music in the form of melody and rhythm. Thus, jazz combos provide alignment at the higher levels of Know-Why and Know-How, leaving it to individual players to determine what note to play when.

Indian classical music is much closer to jazz than to Western classical music. There is no written score in Indian music. In fact, Indian classic music is even more unbound than jazz because there are no set melodies either! Yet Indian classical music ensembles can play together harmoniously for hours. It is always evident that the ensembles are improvising, yet they are coordinated. The coordination between players in an Indian classical music combo is obtained from musical structures, the 'raga' and the 'tala'. These structures are even more simple and fundamental than the coordination structures of jazz. The tala corresponds loosely to rhythm in Western music, while the raga is a simple arrangement of a few notes. The players work with the raga and the tala to weave rich tapestries of music for hours even.

What is it that Indian musicians are tuned to, if not a written score, or a melody, that enables them to coordinate even as they innovate? Here is what a leading practitioner of Indian music says. Amjad Ali Khan is a maestro of the sarod, a multi-stringed instrument that is played by plucking the strings. He was on stage in Mumbai one evening with his two sons, both of whom are also accomplished sarod players. With them were the mandatory accompaniments to any concert of classical Indian music—a tabla maestro beside them, and a tanpura player behind them. The audience was eagerly looking forward to a very special experience of three masters of the sarod playing together.

Amjad Ali Khan and his sons settled on stage in front of their audience. Their first act was the tuning of their instruments, a regular warm-up routine in Indian classical music concerts. Amjad Ali Khan leaned over to the tanpura player behind him, and held his ears close to the tanpura. He then leaned towards the instruments of his sons. They all fiddled with the tuning knobs on their instruments, as they plucked away, looking at each other for confirmation that they had found the sound they wanted to hear.

Then the maestro spoke to the audience. 'Indian music is the sound of a pure voice,' he said. 'A voice that the musician has in his head and that he wishes to hear. He has a yearning for that pure voice, and he plays his instrument to produce it.'

Ending this chapter on a note of music, we enter the realm of measurements in the next chapter. 'What you cannot measure you cannot manage' is a popular saying. We have gone too far in applying this notion in economics and we may go too far when we extend this to human affairs. By putting everything into measured boxes, we can destroy a system's ability to create innovations and to evolve. Math is good, but so is music.

5

MONITORING AND CONTROLLING

And each year, we discover a few more of these unknown unknowns… There's another way to phrase that and that is that the absence of evidence is not evidence of absence.

—DONALD RUMSFELD

The theme of the annual meeting in 2013 of the Global Economic Symposium, which is organized annually by the Kiel Institute for the World Economy, was 'Redefining Success'. Three hundred economists, social scientists and policymakers from many countries convened to examine the prevalent paradigms of economic growth.

Prof Dennis J. Snower, president of the Kiel Institute, opened the meeting with a stirring account of three narratives of economic development that are converging. The first is the mainstream 'materialistic progress narrative'. In this narrative, economic growth, measured principally as growth in gross domestic product (GDP), benefits everybody in the long run. Propelled by this paradigm of progress, the GDP of many developing countries has increased rapidly in the last two decades. Along with this growth, principally in the billion-plus population countries, viz. China and India, the numbers of people below the poverty line globally has reduced by one billion. In this paradigm, without growth of

GDP, there can be no progress. So economists and policymakers are trying to find ever new ways to stimulate growth. Individual initiatives, free markets and private sector activities are considered the essential, and perhaps even the only, drivers of growth. Governments seem to come in the way and have to be kept at bay.

The second narrative is the 'global risk narrative'. This has gained strength in the last fifteen years or so, principally on account of the looming fear of inexorable climate change caused by the excessive carbon spewed into the atmosphere by relentless material and energy consumption. Risks to the sustainability of economic growth on account of these 'externalities' are now realized. It is becoming clear that the present paradigm of growth is not sustainable. Because if everyone in the world were to have the lifestyles present in the West, with the same material consumption levels, we would need four or five additional earths by 2050 to support everyone! Other externalities of the materialistic growth narrative are increasing inequalities within countries—inequalities of income and, more worrying, inequalities of access to opportunities. Not only are these of great concern from a moral perspective, increasing inequalities limit economic growth too, according to some economists, and therefore are risks to growth that must be managed.

The third narrative is the 'happiness narrative'. It was always known to most people outside the hard core economics fraternity that human beings are not satisfied merely with material progress. They seek something more, something ephemeral. Some call this 'happiness', others call it 'well-being'. It is not clear how to define these qualities exactly, or how to measure them. Therefore, the challenge for economists and policymakers is to expand their measurement models and policy frameworks to include these intangibles in a tangible way. Indeed some countries have begun to do this.

Prof Snower concluded with a memorable statement: 'We plunder our planet to produce more material goods in pursuit of pleasures that fail to materialize.' The two-day symposium, with dozens of parallel sessions, buzzed with ideas for the integration of the three narratives. At the closing plenary, seven persons on a panel were asked what thoughts they had on how to do this.

The economists amongst them said that unless one can measure something one cannot manage it. We are having a difficult time, as it is, trying to estimate and manage economies, they said. Therefore, we must be cautious when we begin to add on other less tangible objectives. Later, the moderator went around asking each of the panelists what they deeply wanted the world to become. One of the economists said he wanted a world in which the dignity of all human beings was enhanced and respected. Which begged the question, of course, how do you measure dignity?

Economists seem caught in the trap of measurement. Even in their own hearts, they hear a music that defies enumeration. What is the way out of the trap? In this chapter we explore the compulsions to measure, not only for economists but also for policymakers and corporate executives. And then we will examine some new ways being developed to understand the goals we are seeking and to manage our progress towards them.

BLINKERS ON THE STUDY OF ECONOMIES

First, we examine the dilemma of economics itself. Mainstream economics has become like an ostrich with its head in the sand, unwilling to see what is around it. Lacking comprehensive models, it is unable to comprehend reality. And its incomplete models cannot be relied upon for accurate predictions. There are too many externalities not included in them.

When the growth of the Indian economy began to decline from

2011, there was a lot of consternation. There were many debates in the media about what was causing the decline and great anxiety about when it would be reversed. As would be expected, the media turned to economists for answers. Most of these debates seemed to be mere babbling speculations about numbers. 'What will be the GDP growth this year?' was the most often asked question. But also, 'What will be the GDP growth for *last* year?' This was because accurate numbers of growth of the Indian economy for any period are available only after a considerable lag. The answers of economists to the first question generally have a ring of authority and certainty: 'I am confident that the growth will be...' However, to answer the second question there is a hesitation: 'Let us wait till the final numbers come in.' (Hoping these may be a little closer to the forecast made earlier which is turning out to have been way off the mark!)

Nate Silver points out, in *The Signal and the Noise* (2012), that forecasts of GDP growth since 1968 by the Survey of Professional Forecasters have been right only 50 per cent of the time—no better than tossing a coin—and that economists have predicted only two out of the sixty recessions in the world since 1990 a year ahead of time. Should we keep turning to economists for guidance if they do not seem to know what is going on? was Queen Elizabeth's concern when she asked why economists could not predict the recent global recession. The problem is that while economists do not have a good model to explain the relationships between the many forces shaping societies and economies, they nevertheless want to sound like experts by adding decimal points to their predictions.

Some economists admit they suffer from physics envy. They aspire to model complex socio-economic phenomena in the way physicists model natural phenomena. Kenneth Arrow and Brian Arthur, Nobel laureates in economics, arranged a meeting of economists in 1987 with physicists, including Nobel laureates Murray Gell-Mann and Phil Anderson, to understand what economists may learn from physicists about the formulation of theories and models. The economists presented their models. M. Mitchel Waldorp gives an account of the meeting in his book, *Complexity: The Emerging Science at the Edge of Order and Chaos* (1992: 140):

> And indeed, as the axioms and theorems and proofs marched across the overhead projector screen, the physicists could only be awestruck at their counterparts' mathematical prowess--awestruck and appalled. They had the same objection that Arthur and many other economists had been voicing from within the field for years. 'They were almost too good,' says one young physicist, who remembers shaking his head in disbelief. 'It seemed as though they were dazzling themselves with fancy mathematics, until they really couldn't see the forest for the trees. So much time was being spent on trying to absorb the mathematics that I thought they weren't often looking at what the models were for, and what they did, and whether the underlying assumptions were any good. In a lot of cases, what was required was just some common sense.'

The pursuit of numbers, in the belief that numbers alone indicate accuracy, has become the bane of economics. Many forces that shape societies and economies cannot be easily measured such as the trust of citizens in institutions. Such substantial forces must not be excluded from a model which seeks to explain the behaviour of the economy. Robert Lucas, who received the Nobel Prize in economics for expounding the 'rational-expectations' view of human behaviour, referred to a theory as something that can be put on a computer and run. Many economists insist on equations and numbers because that is all that computers can compute, whereas economists should study human behaviour as it is, not as they find easy to model.

British economist Adair Turner, delivering the 2010 Lionel Robbins Memorial Lectures, said the time has come to reconstruct economics. Too much reality was being left out of economists' models for them to explain the world. These flawed models are incapable of predicting the future condition of an economy. With a twist of Keynes' famous statement, that 'practical men, who believe themselves to be quite exempt from any intellectual influences, are usually the slaves of some defunct economist', Turner warns that 'the great danger lies with reasonably intellectual men and women who are employed in the policy-making departments of central banks, regulatory bodies, and governments, who are aware of intellectual influences, but who tend to gravitate to simplified versions of the dominant beliefs of economists who are still very much alive' (Turner 2012).

Economists have been the emperors of government policy in most countries in the last twenty years. There is plenty of evidence that their models and calculations are inaccurate. The *exposé* in 2013 of the flaw in the calculus of Prof Rogoff and Prof Reinhart (of the relationship between deficits and growth) was an embarrassing sign that the emperor is not well clothed. Economists need to be humble, Turner says. They must no longer attribute economic problems only to politicians' lack of will to implement the solutions that economists insist on.

The reconstruction of economics will require the inclusion of many disciplines of social and ecological sciences in a collaborative inquiry. Human societies and economies are complex systems. To see the whole elephant, those who have blinded themselves to others' points of view by their conceptual and ideological differences must come together. The first step to build a better model, before writing equations and running the computations, is to prepare a diagram—a map of the whole system. Mathematical maps of economies that give the exact sizes of the few features they can measure, leaving out all other features, are not useful. For a map to be a useful guide for a journey, all rivers and mountains must be represented in it, even if their exact widths and heights are not yet known.

PLANNING AND THE STATE

In his book, *Seeing Like a State*, James Scott (1998: 11) says:

> Certain forms of knowledge and control require a narrowing of vision. The great advantage of such tunnel vision is that it brings into sharp focus certain limited aspects of an otherwise far more complex and unwieldy reality. This very simplification, in turn, makes the phenomenon in the center of the field of vision more legible and hence more susceptible to careful measurement and calculation.

We have already discussed the narrow vision of mainstream economics. Scott points out that not only do certain forms of *knowledge* require a narrowing of vision, but that certain forms of *control* also require a narrowing of vision. He also introduces the need for *legibility*, required for both knowledge and control. While economists may be interested only in understanding and explaining how an economy works, policymakers and state managers are expected to control the economy and to manipulate it to produce required outcomes.

Economists simplify systems to make them legible for themselves, as we saw earlier. State and business managers also simplify systems to efficiently get the information they need to control and manipulate systems, as we shall now see. And when economists, with their oversimplified models of very complex systems, guide state managers to take bold actions, there is great risk that the combination may have bad consequences. This was the principal cause for the failure of the Soviet system of state planning.

Let us examine why the narrowness of state and business models for managing complex systems has bad consequences. Following Scott's line of argument, we will look at the management of forests, cities and larger state systems.

Forests

'Scientific forestry' was introduced in the 18th century in Prussia and Saxony. Its objectives were to increase the yield of forests for commercial purposes and enable the state to efficiently manage its revenues from the extraction of timber. The focus was on the timber in the trees in the forest, to the exclusion of all other paraphernalia around it—the bushes, shrubs, grasses, animals, and insects. Everything else other than those species of trees that were valuable for timber was interference to the timber enterprise. These hindrances also occupied valuable forest space. Therefore, scientific forestry promoted monoculture of single species of trees. Moreover, by planting them in even rows, the counting of the trees and estimation of the timber content of the forest was simplified; also simplified was the care of the trees when necessary and their felling too. As Scott describes it: 'The forest as a habitat disappears to be replaced by the forest as an economic resource to be managed efficiently and profitably.' (ibid.)

The elimination of the diversity of the forest, by removing flora and fauna of no interest for commerce and taxes for the state, made these forests less resilient to environmental changes, and thus their yields reduced over time, and to maintain them required more inputs of resources by their managers. Also, the removal of the bushes and trees that were not valuable for timber deprived people who depended on these for their livelihoods. Therefore, forestry for commercial and state purposes often will be resisted by those who live in and around forests, as is the case in the large forest tracts in India which have been habitats of tribal people for centuries.

Scientific agriculture follows the pattern of scientific forestry. Large fields are planted with a single variety of plant. These plants are valuable 'crops' that are fertilized and protected. All other plants in the field are dismissed as unnecessary weeds. Thus, in fields and forests, 'nature' is converted into 'natural resources' for human enterprises.

Cities

Turning to cities, Scott contrasts the approaches of modern city planners with the more organic approaches of urbanists such as Jane Jacobs whose work on institutional architectures was referred to in Chapter 3 (Jacobs 1994). The archetype of the high modernist city planner for Scott is Le Corbusier, who designed and laid out the green field city of Chandigarh in northern India in the 1960s.

Le Corbusier had a vision of mechanical order. Each part of the city was designed for a specific purpose: some parts for residences of the elite, others for residences of those with lesser incomes, some parts for markets, and others for offices. Mixed use would make it difficult to produce the functional efficiency in the parts that Le Corbusier wanted. As Scott (1998) reports, Le Corbusier said: 'Faced with a labyrinth of possibilities the human mind loses itself and becomes fatigued.' For him a home was 'a machine for living in'. He had calculated the optimum amount of space that each type of human being needed for various purposes and just that was to be provided. He put people into boxes, assigning spaces for standard categories of activities. In each box—zones and dwellings—the requirements for that category of activity could be scientifically provided. On the other hand, mixing up categories would result in interactions which would introduce complexity for the planner.

Le Corbusier's dictum was, 'The Plan: the Dictator!' Like the scientific forester who reduced the chaos of natural forests, Le Corbusier contrasted existing cities which were the complicated products of historical chance with his vision of cities of the future which would be consciously designed from start to finish following scientific principles.

While Le Corbusier viewed the macro order of cities from above, Jane Jacobs viewed the micro order of cities from the perspective of people on the ground. She observed the patterns of their actions and interactions, and observed how the physical structures of cities enabled or hindered them. Le Corbusier saw a visual order; Jacobs saw an experienced order.

Scott quotes Stanley Tankel, another urbanist, with Jacob's humanist perspective, who said: 'It is beyond the scope of anyone's imagination to create a community. We must learn to cherish the communities we have, they are hard to come by.' Tankel opposed large-scale slum removal. 'Fix the buildings but leave the people,' he said (ibid.: 144).

One of the mega trends of the 21st century according to all futurists will be rapid urbanization. Billions of people in the developing countries living in rural settings will hereafter live in urban conglomerations. Some of this growth in urban populations will be by the migration of people to urban conglomerations from rural areas in search of better livelihoods. In densely populated countries such as India, urbanization will also increase with the organic growth of rural settlements that become denser and change to urban conglomerations.

Urbanization is a major force propelling economic growth. Urban aggregations create economic efficiencies and, by connecting many diverse talents and activities, are fertile sources of innovations too. Thus urban conglomerations create opportunities for employment and enterprise that were not available in less dense and less diverse rural areas. Therefore, in addition to the growth of GDP, they are also a means for more inclusive growth.

Many Indians, seeing the transformation of the infrastructure of cities in Asia—in Singapore, Kuala Lumpur and Shanghai—would like their cities to become 'world class' too. They contrast the experience of travelling from the airports in these cities to the city centres within their own cities such as Mumbai. Some say they are ashamed that foreign tourists and business people visiting Mumbai have to pass so many slums, whereas cities such as Shanghai have seemingly got rid of their slums.

'What is a world class city?' asks urbanist Jeb Brugmann in his book, *Welcome to the Urban Revolution* (2009). He describes a scientific way to answer this question. First, lay down the criteria and then compare cities objectively against the criteria. He says that if, as economists seem to agree, cities provide the best means for people to increase their incomes compared to opportunities in rural settings, then *those cities that have enabled the largest numbers of rural migrants to increase their incomes, with the least amount of public investments*, are the most effective at fulfilling the primary purpose of cities in the course of economic growth. He then compares cities around the world against this criterion.

The winner according to Brugmann is the congested, bustling square mile in the middle of Mumbai, inhabited by a million people, called Dharavi. Dharavi, he says, 'is probably the most successful, scaled poverty-reduction program in the history of international development. Dharavi's migrant generations have developed an accessible, replicable citysystem for the advancement of the country's poor majority. It is a stunning example of Indian entrepreneurial ability and ambition' (ibid.: 135). Dharavi's core residents were poor migrants from many parts of India who set up small enterprises in a variety of industries including leather, garments, food processing, light engineering, and electronic assembly. The total turnover of the small enterprises within Dharavi is estimated at over US$500 million. Dharavi exports goods around the world.

Brugmann describes his shock when he was shown plans made by a successful Indian-American mansion builder from the US to remove the Dharavi 'slum' which was an eyesore for the Indians who wanted Mumbai to be transformed into a 'world-class city'. Dharavi looks like a slum because its inhabitants do not have adequate sanitation and water services. They are considered illegal occupants of the land and are denied the municipal services provided to others in Mumbai. Rather than provide them with basic services, the plan would displace them, disrupt their web of interdependent enterprises, to make room for aesthetically acceptable modern buildings. The scheme would put Dharavi's entrepreneurial citizens into boxes designed by an architect who would never be able to map the myriad social and business interactions that made Dharavi hum.

According to the 2011 census, 377 million Indians were living in towns and cities in 2011. It is projected that there will be 600 million by 2030, an increase of over 200 million in twenty years. India has to be prepared for this new urban expansion along with a huge backlog of infrastructure and services to be provided to many millions of Indians living in slum-like conditions, like the citizens of Dharavi. The government's urban programmes were focused on the improvement of the large metropolises. Moreover, the approach of planners so far has been to focus on the physical infrastructure, relocation of slums, and provision of new housing. Cities were provided financial assistance from the central government for projects prepared by qualified city planners. Sadly, these plans were hardly ever endorsed by the citizens on the ground.

A new sensibility is beginning to inform plans for India's urbanization. It has been realized that the growth of urban conglomerations is happening in peri-urban areas around cities, not in them, and also in small towns that are organically growing into larger ones. There can be no standard template of urban design for these diverse conglomerations. Each is growing organically within its own geography and following its own history. In the second phase of India's national urban renewal mission, the Jawaharlal Nehru National Urban Renewal Mission (JNNURM) II, cities are required to prepare their own spatial plans combining the physical, economic and social developments of the city. Citizen participation in the preparation of the plans is mandated. Templates to make the plans are being provided and assistance to facilitate their preparation will be given.

The approach to city planning is changing from an engineer's master plans, like Le Corbusier's, made from above to the organic, composite plans made with inputs from the citizens on the streets, as Jacobs, Brugmann and others have been advocating. The change in perspective and the approach to planning has not been easy. Qualified experts in city planning say common citizens do not understand what city planning is about. Those advocating the new approach reply that the experts do not know what the city is about. In the end, the talents of the experts and the citizens must be combined. Experts must respond to the requirements of the citizens and build on their insights too.

The State, Planning and Control

James Scott's central thesis, expressed in the title of his book, *Seeing Like a State* (1998), is that the state needs the means to make its territories and citizens 'legible'. It must know who they are, where they live, what they own, what they do. It needs this information for benign purposes of efficiently collecting taxes and providing them services, and also for less benign purposes of keeping an eye on them.

Gathering information can be a costly exercise. Therefore, the state must find ways to reduce its costs. It finds criteria for dividing citizens into categories appropriate for its purposes. A classic example of this is the 'door and window tax' system introduced in France in the 19th century. Property taxes due were proportional to the area of each house. Measuring each house's area was a difficult exercise for tax assessors. An ingenious solution was found. Larger houses are expected to have more doors and windows. So tax assessors could walk around the house and count the numbers of doors and windows and determine the tax due!

People figured this out. New houses were then built with fewer openings in their outside walls. This resulted in the peculiar design of houses still seen in the French countryside. The ingenious tax collection system became ineffective. The door and window tax system was abolished in 1917. However, an unintended consequence of the system was the deterioration of the health of citizens stuffed into houses with poor ventilation, the cost of which to society was perhaps larger than the taxes lost by the state.

The adage that one can only manage what one measures had taken a new twist. When measurement is focused on only one part of the system, the system itself can be distorted! Indeed, this may be a consequence of many measurement systems including the measurement of GDP, which improves the GDP but causes undesirable side effects on the environment and society.

Efficiency of measurement necessitates simplification and focus on what can be measured. What is measurable and included in economists' models are the endogenous variables. What is fuzzy is inconvenient and is excluded. The variables excluded are exogenous to their model economists say and that is that. These variables may be exogenous to economists' models and policymakers' schemes but they remain an inherent part of the system. They will strike into the model thus distorting what is measured too.

Isaiah Berlin says in his treatise, 'On Political Judgement' (1996):

> All socially engineered systems of formal order are in fact subsystems of a larger system on which they are ultimately dependent, not to say parasitic. The subsystem relies on a variety of processes—frequently informal or antecedent—which alone it cannot create or maintain. The more schematic, thin, and simplified the formal order, the less resilient and more vulnerable it is to distortions outside its narrow parameters.

Systems' modellers know that all significant forces that affect each other must be included in the description of the system even if they cannot be numerically measured with available techniques. Therefore, systems' models used for creating scenarios that can provide reliable explanations of what may happen in the future must include forces such as citizens' trust in institutions. Declining trust, as we saw in the India scenarios in Chapter 2, can have a large effect on the growth of India's GDP. Economists using incomplete models have been trying to predict India's GDP growth and have been getting it very wrong in the last few years because they do not factor in such forces.

LEARNING TO MEASURE WHAT WE REALLY WANT

Let us return to the Global Economic Symposium in Kiel with which I opened this chapter. The symposium began with a call for new scorecards for measuring progress. It was admitted that economic measures alone will not do. The symposium ended with a call for good leadership to change the trajectory of human progress. And all agreed that we need leaders with good heads and good hearts. Therefore, leaders may have to learn to measure what they aspire for in their hearts too.

At the closing plenary, an economist had said that he wanted most of all a world in which everyone lived in dignity. How can one measure dignity? How do people experience dignity? Or, the absence of it in their own lives?

A principal objective of India's 12th Five Year Plan is to achieve inclusive growth. Growth is measured as the growth of GDP. How does one measure inclusion? To understand inclusion, one must listen to those who are excluded to understand how they experience their exclusion. In the run-up to the 12th Plan, the Planning Commission had given an open invitation to representatives of all groups who are voicing their exclusion from India's growth— dalits, minorities, tribals, women, the physically challenged, etc. Thus some 950 civil society organizations (CSOs) participated in a process of consultation. In one of the meetings, an attractive woman stood up, and spoke in a man's voice! There was shocked silence in the room. She said: 'We trans-genders are humans too. Millions of us in the country are shunned from your imaginations.'

In a TV debate on 'Is India an Inclusive Nation', after an economist had recited numbers about the reduction of poverty, a well-dressed young man with Mongoloid features, speaking perfect English, stood up. He recounted his experience of exclusion. When he arrived for a job interview in an office in Delhi he was turned away by the security guard with the snub, 'There is no work for you here, bahadur.' ('Bahadur' is a term often used pejoratively in Delhi to address persons with Mongoloid features.)

A measure of income alone cannot be an indicator of exclusion. The quality of inclusion is a relative experience, and a moving target. How much a community has been included in a society can be judged by the ways in which its members feel excluded by others. Moreover, the measure of inclusion will always be a moving target in any developing nation. As the nation's GDP and average per capita income increase, the poor may have more income and consumption in absolute terms than they had before. But unless there is absolute equality, some will always have more and others less, and those with less will feel relatively poor. How much inequality a nation will tolerate within itself is a critical measure of the inclusive quality of the nation.

In their book *The Spirit Level* (2009) Richard Wilkinson and Kate Pickett assess the consequences of inequality in nations on several measures of well-being, such as public health and crime, and even on the sustainability of economic growth rates. In his 2010 Hugo Young Lecture, David Cameron, Britain's prime minister, said *The Spirit Level* showed that,

> Amongst the richest countries, it is the most unequal ones that do worse on almost every quality of life indicator… per capita GDP is much less significant for a country's life expectancy, crime levels, literacy and health than the size of the gap between the richest and poorest in the population…We all know in our hearts, that as long as there is deep poverty living systematically side by side with great riches, we will all remain poorer for it.

Concepts of economic growth aim to increase total GDP and per capita income. They are driven by a utilitarian concept of justice, in which it is acceptable if some must be sacrificed for the progress of the majority. On the other hand, a humanitarian concept of justice will not accept that anyone should suffer for the benefit of another. In her book *Righteous Republic: The Political Foundations of Modern India* (2012), Ananya Vajpeyi relates a story from the

Mahabharata. When Yudhisthra meets his father Dharma who is disguised as a Yaksha (a heavenly being), the Yaksha asks him a series of questions which he must answer correctly to get back the life of his temporarily deceased brothers. Yudhisthra answers them correctly. He is under the impression that only one brother can be saved. When asked which one he would chose, he picks Nakula, his half-brother. The Yaksha is surprised. Yudhisthra explains that his mother, Kunti, already has a living son—Yudhisthra himself— whereas his stepmother, Madri, has only one son, Nakula, and it would be cruel to deprive her of a son. The Yaksha is so pleased with Yudhisthra's inclusive concept of justice that he revives all his brothers!

India is the world's largest democracy in terms of population. Its Constitution granted political equality to all citizens, men and women, regardless of their incomes and levels of education, even before some Western countries did. However, as Dr Bhimrao Ambedkar, the leading architect of India's Constitution realized, inclusion cannot be legislated into a society. It requires deep changes in attitudes and institutions. He turned to Buddhism for solutions and aspired to convert the mission of Buddhism from a path for personal salvation to a path for societal salvation. Buddhism teaches that dukha (suffering) is a permanent condition in a person's life. Ambedkar, experiencing the persistent inequities built into social institutions, suggested that dukha is a permanent condition in a society too. Compassion for others, as Yudhisthra illustrated, is the way out of dukha for individuals and society.

The challenge for economists is that inclusion cannot be measured by an absolute poverty line. Inclusion must be measured by inequality too. And inequality cannot be measured in economic terms alone. Assessments of the many ways in which exclusion is experienced by communities and individuals are also necessary.

If we can manage only what we can measure, then economists

and planners must determine, though it is not easy, how inclusion and dignity can be gauged and measured to make plans to achieve fully inclusive growth with dignity for all. To know what inclusion and dignity mean, we must listen to the experiences of diverse people. We must ask them how they experience the absence of inclusion, that is exclusion, and the absence of dignity in their lives.

The need to listen and to design processes that facilitate listening appear again in the following chapters on new scorecards, on structures of democracy, and the processes of rebuilding trust in business and government institutions.

6

REDEFINING SUCCESS: NEW SCORECARDS

But yield who will to that temptation,
My object in living is to unite
My avocation and my vocation
As my two eyes make one in sight.

—Robert Frost

Institutions are systems that humanity designs to enable it to reach its aspirations. The essence of institutions is expressed in the norms, the written and unwritten rules, and the patterns of behaviour of members of the institution.

Like aeroplanes and rockets, often institutions need to be redesigned to suit new conditions in which they must produce results. Crews flying an aeroplane need gauges to let them know where the aeroplane is heading and to monitor the aeroplane's operating systems. Without instruments on the dashboard the crew cannot manage the flight of the aeroplane. This is another way of saying, as economists and policymakers often do, that you can manage only what you can measure. Scorecards of the performance of a country, or a business, are like the cluster of instruments in the cockpit of an aeroplane. This chapter is about designing scorecards for managing a business corporation and for guiding the progress of a country.

Designers of scorecards for institutions should always keep two things in mind. One is that the process of measurement can change the behaviour of the people in the institution. The second critical requirement for designing institutional scorecards is to always keep in mind the purpose for which the institution was created.

Measurement of the behaviours of people in an organization makes them change their patterns of behaviour. This is like the Heisenberg Principle of Uncertainty in physics, whereby the process of measurement changes what is being measured. Some of the changes caused by measurement would be changes that the managers of the institution desire. However, the measurements may also induce changes that are not desired, as was the effect of the door and window tax in France (described in the previous chapter).

I have experienced the influence of measurements on my own behaviour when I moved from India to the United States (US) in 1989. I had worked for twenty-five years with the Tata Group in India. While I was working my way up the company hierarchy from the 1960s till the 1980s, the ethic was to build the country, an ethic that the Tata Group of companies exemplified. The making and spending of large amounts of money by individuals was frowned upon. Salaries of board members of large companies were curbed by law to be not more than the salaries of top-level Indian civil servants—which were much less than the salaries of civil servants in other countries.

I was amongst the best compensated executives in India. I was well satisfied and not aware of how little I was paid compared to international levels. However, I had earned and saved very little compared to much younger executives of US companies even though I had been at the board level of my company for many years.

When I moved to the US in 1989, I had no savings at all with which to set myself up in a new country, to buy a car and a house. Even if I had saved enough money in India, I could not have taken it with me to the US because, until the economic reforms of the 1990s, taking money out of India was forbidden. I could afford only a small used car and a small rented apartment to start life in the Boston area with the consulting company I joined, while even much younger consultants in the company owned two cars and large homes.

The consulting company had an elaborate performance measurement system which quantified the contributions of partners and consultants and which had precise formulae for their monetary compensation. The company gave large monetary rewards for good performance. This was the way in the US—high performance must result in high monetary rewards. The measure of your success was the amount of money you made.

Having done very well professionally in India I was respected for my experience by the young consultants. A few months after I began work, a young American consultant who had worked with me on some difficult engagements in which my experience had proven valuable to the company's clients, asked me a candid question. He said, 'I believe you are very good at what we do. But how come if you are so good, you are not rich?' He left unstated the real concern on his mind, which was: if I was not rich, perhaps I was not really good!

I needed to earn more to live better and to be financially more secure. Soon I was learning to play by the written rules of the performance management system. I was being subtly brainwashed to adopt the norm on which the system was based, that more money is what one works for, and not the intrinsic rewards of the work, which had been a strong norm in the India I had left.

THE EVOLUTION OF THE BUSINESS CORPORATION

Institutions are the vehicles with which humanity achieves its aspirations. When the conditions in which human societies must sustain themselves change, or when new aspirations arise, the evolution of new institutions becomes necessary. Two principal sets of institutions that humanity has designed for its economic and social progress are institutions of business and institutions of government. Scorecards must be congruent with the purpose the institution is required to serve for society.

Ronald Reagan said that government is not the solution for the progress of societies. It is the problem, he said. Like Margaret Thatcher in the United Kingdom (UK), he gave more freedom to financial and business corporations. Like Thatcher, he trampled on labour unions and rolled back government regulations coming in the way of corporations' freedoms.

The excessive rolling back of government by 'Reagonomics' contributed to the recent financial crisis in the US, which has shaken the global economy: a shock from which it has yet to recover. The US government did too little to prevent the crisis, its critics now say. It should have tamed the animal spirits in the market. Let us now examine the nature of the beast that was to be tamed, viz. financial and business corporations.

The limited liability corporation is an invention of man: a device created to attract capital. The liabilities of investors are limited to encourage them to invest and take risks with their capital. The East India Company, established in AD 1600, was one of the first 'limited liability corporations' in the world. Its owners contributed capital for the voyages of the company's ships to the East and, later, for its ventures in India. The owners shared the profits of the ventures amongst themselves.

The records of meetings of the East India Company's Board

in London in the 17th and 18th centuries reveal that the directors were only concerned about calculating the profits and their distribution amongst the shareholders. They seemed hardly aware of the violence and corruption in the conduct of their employees in India. What the company's employees did to earn the profits for the owners was of little concern to them.

The tenet driving the conduct of the East India Company was 'the business of business must be only business'. The rest was none of their business. The resentment of India's people to the conduct of the company led to the War of Independence in 1857. Combined with the reactions to the conduct of the East India Company of high-minded societal leaders in Britain, this resulted in the British government taking over the company's affairs in India.

Ted Nace, in an excellent book, albeit with a provocative title, *Gangs of America: The Rise of Corporate Power and the Disabling of Democracy* (2003), records that, a very few years later, in 1864, Abraham Lincoln wrote these words after the American Civil War:

> I see in the future a crisis approaching that unnerves me and causes me to tremble for the future of my country. As a result of the war, corporations have been enthroned and an era of corruption in high places will follow, and the money power of the country will endeavor to prolong its reign by working upon the prejudices of the people until all wealth is aggregated in a few hands and the Republic is destroyed.

Over the next 150 years, through a series of legal and ideological battles in the US, corporations acquired all the rights of citizens to protection of properties and other freedoms. In addition, they obtained privileges of limited liability and other protections that human citizens do not have. This history has been documented by Ted Nace in his book cited above. Laws were made whereby corporations could privatize and internalize profits, while costs of damages to communities and the environment were socialized and externalized.

However, the principle that 'the business of business must be only business' has continued to guide corporate conduct into the 20th century, especially in the Anglo-Saxon world, reinforced by the philosophy of Nobel laureate Milton Friedman and the Chicago School of Economics. The responsibility of the board of a company, according to this philosophy, is to ensure that shareholder value is increased and that disbursement of profits to the shareholders is equitable.

Many US business corporations amassed huge profits for their principal owners in the 19th and 20th centuries, some of whom created trusts in their names that have gone on to do excellent philanthropic work. However, the damage that some of these companies had done to the environment and communities in the course of making their profits, as well as societal and political reactions to their monopolist and corrupt practices, led to political pressure to create laws to regulate corporate conduct.

By the end of the 20th century, the world had changed dramatically compared to the conditions in which the East India Company had operated, and even the conditions in which 20th century corporations have operated. An increasing awareness of fundamental human rights, the realization that economic activity was damaging the environment too much, and the ubiquity of information available to citizens has begun to put great pressure on corporations to change their ways. Society has begun to demand a new code of business responsibility in return for granting corporations their licenses to operate. Powered by global communication networks, this demand has grown in both the developed and the developing world.

The context in which corporations must now operate has

changed dramatically. Therefore, the concept of what their responsibility is to society and what their governance practices should be must change too. The business of business can no longer be just business. New institutions are required. A new form of business corporation must evolve.

THE DEATH OF OLD-FASHIONED CORPORATE SOCIAL RESPONSIBILITY (CSR) AND THE BIRTH OF BUSINESS RESPONSIBILITY

The damage, or benefit, for society and the environment is caused by a company's operations and products. What it does afterwards with a portion of those profits to repair the damage caused can only be a small token. Therefore, societal attention is shifting from how business profits are used after they are made to how the profits are made in the first place.

An exaggerated example will help to explain the new concept of business responsibility that leaders are now promoting. There is a large demand for hard drugs in many parts of the world. A businessman can seize this opportunity and produce and sell such drugs to make large profits, and damage many lives in the process. He may then use a portion of the profits to set up the world's best clinics to rehabilitate drug addicts. By spending this money on a very worthy cause has he fulfilled his corporate social responsibility (CSR)?

This question is not as far-fetched as an example of a company selling hard drugs may make it appear. Companies that sell cigarettes, companies that destroy forests and displace tribal people to mine ores, and armament producers, all contribute to the destruction of the lives of people with their products and operations. How much of the damage can they repair by spending a small portion of their profits on 'CSR'? Societies are increasingly demanding explanations on how the 100 per cent of revenues were produced, and not the glowing accounts of the small percentages of profits that were spent on CSR.

Profit is a small fraction of the revenues and costs of a business, perhaps no more than 10 per cent in most cases. The 2 per cent of profits spent on CSR (which a new Indian law mandates) will be only 0.2 per cent of a company's revenues. Hundred per cent of the revenues is the impact of the corporate Titanic on the environment and communities through which it traverses. Spending 0.2 per cent of revenues on CSR is like rearranging the deck chairs on the Titanic. Socially responsible corporations in the 21st century must account to society for the impact of their operations and products on the health of citizens and on the condition of societies and communities. Spending a small amount of profits on philanthropy and CSR is no longer an acceptable way to win societal trust.

Corporations cannot be isolated from the larger natural and social systems of which they are a part. Whether they are sensitive to it or not, corporations interact with the world around them in the following five domains:

- Accountability to investors and lenders—the financial domain; and the domain of corporate accounting, auditing, corporate law, and stock market regulators. So far this has been the principal focus of corporate governance.
- Accountability to the direct participants in the corporate value creation process—customers, employees, vendors. This is the domain of consumer protection laws, labour laws and laws for commercial contracts. Along with the first domain, this has been the principal focus of corporate management.
- Accountability for the effect of their operations on the physical environment. This is the domain of environmental regulations

which are pinching corporations now.
- Accountability for the human condition around their operations—health, education, employment, and cultural needs in the community. Here corporate responsibility is not much regulated. So far this has been a principal domain for corporate philanthropy.
- Accountability for the political health of the societies in which they operate—the implementation of human rights, fair democratic practices, etc. This is the new frontier of business responsibility. It sees corporations as citizens in their societies with responsibility to shape and support societal norms. Should corporations be merely takers of permissions from society or should they not contribute to creating fair conditions for all citizens?

These five domains are like steps of a ladder of business responsibility.

The first two rungs of the ladder are simply good management of the business of business. If corporations do not manage their relationships with their investors well they can be squeezed out of existence. If they do not manage their relations with stakeholders in their direct value-production chains—employees, customers, distributors, and vendors—they cannot produce value for their investors and they risk going out of business. Many corporate report cards on CSR and business responsibility report innovations in managing relationships with employees, customers and small vendors. These are stuck within the paradigm that the business of business is only business. They do not stretch models of business responsibility sufficiently.

The third and fourth rungs of the ladder lift corporate governance higher. In these domains, corporations must examine the impact of their operations and products on communities and the natural environment. It is in these domains of responsibility that old-fashioned CSR and philanthropy—spending a portion of profits on societal and environmental concerns—diverge from the new paradigm of business responsibility to account for the impact of the corporation's entire operations and products.

Triple Bottom Line performance measurement and People-Planet-Profits reports are innovations at the third and fourth levels of the business responsibility ladder. They require 'balanced scorecards' to report the corporation's economic, social and environmental performance.

There is a fifth rung too. To get a perspective of business responsibility from this level, let us consider two egregious cases.

In 2002, several thousand people, mostly Muslims, were massacred in riots in the state of Gujarat in India. Many members of the Confederation of Indian Industry (CII) were disturbed by the human misery. In a national meeting in Delhi they discussed whether the carnage in Gujarat could have been prevented had Indian business leaders been more actively engaged in sociopolitical developments in the country. Participating in a heated debate on the role of the Gujarat government in this meeting, a spokesperson of the Bharatiya Janata Party (BJP), which was ruling the state of Gujarat at the time, wondered why industry was making a noise about the mayhem in Gujarat when it had remained silent when Hindus had been driven out of Kashmir some years earlier. Trying to turn the tables on industry, he suggested the Gujarat riots might not have happened had industry intervened in earlier communal problems such as those in Kashmir.

Similarly, Royal Dutch Shell was accused of complicity by remaining silent when the Nigerian government executed Ken Saro-Wiwa, the Nigerian writer and environmental activist. Shell was in a quandary at the time. Its business philosophy was to be a good corporate citizen and to work in 'partnership' with local governments everywhere. But what if the government is not effective in protecting human rights? According to Shell's critics, the company should have stood up for what was right in Nigeria even if its business suffered.

With human tragedies, such as those in Nigeria and Gujarat, the debate on the role of corporations in influencing broader sociopolitical change surfaces again. For some business leaders, the question is no longer *whether* business has a role in social change, but *how* it should play its role.

Business corporations must now face up to their broader role in society. In the latter part of the 20th century, markets rather than governments were considered a better way to manage the economies of nations. By the end of the century, the idea of using government-led industrial policies to grow economies had been rubbished. The balance of power in economies had shifted from governments to corporations. Now a backlash is brewing. The power and freedoms of business will be curbed if they do not act responsibly towards a wider set of societal stakeholders. Even in the US, a bastion of free markets, the self-interestedness of corporations and their leaders has caused a reaction.

The environment and concerns of the community were the first two domains of corporate responsibility added to economic measures in 'balanced' corporate scorecards. Sensing wider societal concerns from the fifth rung of the corporate responsibility ladder, good governance is now being added as a fourth category.

The concept of good corporate governance so far has mostly been restricted to the management of a corporation's responsibility to shareholders. Transparency and accuracy in reporting the performance, and the risks to it, to investors, and fairness in dealing with small and minority shareholders have been the principal features of good corporate governance. As would be expected, many studies have shown that corporations with good corporate governance with respect to the concerns of investors are more valued in stock markets.

Now the concept of good corporate governance is becoming broader, as corporations climb up the rungs of the ladder of responsibility, to even responsibility for the impact of the corporation's conduct on the governance of the country. This is conceptually much more difficult to define and measure. Indeed, it is often seen that corporations who twist and even corrupt government processes can produce more value for their shareholders. The benefits of corruption are internalized, whereas the harm they do to the governance of society is externalized. This highlights yet again the corporate governance conundrum. What is the board of a corporation accountable for and who is it accountable to? If it is accountable only to the shareholders (the 'owners') and for producing more value for them, then why should it be concerned about the external costs of producing more shareholder value?

Mahatma Gandhi had reminded business leaders of their deeper relationship with society. He said leaders of corporations were 'trustees' of a society's wealth. As corporate leaders climb up the rungs of the CSR ladder, they come closer and closer to redefining the purpose of the corporation in society. The purpose of the corporation shifts from being merely a vehicle for improving returns for investors, which was the intent of creating limited liability companies, to being a trustee of humanity's natural and social wealth.

In response to the need to account to society, and not just to shareholders, several new ideas have emerged. The movement gaining the most support is the United Nations (UN) Global Compact, which completed its tenth year in 2013. Started by Kofi Annan, then the UN Secretary General, it is the only UN organization that does not have any governmental representation.

It is a voluntary organization run by business leaders from around the world along with representatives of civil society—labour unions, environmental groups, Transparency International, etc.—to institute a universal corporate code of conduct.

The first attention of these corporate leaders was directed towards the environmental impact of businesses. Then the attention moved to determine the impact of business operations and products on the community. Next was added the impact of business conduct on the fabric of polities and societies by corruption and lack of transparency. The principal thrust of UN Global Compact is to encourage and enable businesses to strengthen their compact with society by transparently reporting the impact of their operations and products. Businesses are encouraged to invite comments to their reports and to discuss these with stakeholders. International communities of Global Compact members transfer good practices around the world.

Several formats for reporting the impact of business have been developed, such as the 'Triple Bottom Line' mentioned before and also an ISO standard. The Global Reporting Initiative (GRI), which has tied up with UN Global Compact, is emerging as the most accepted framework. In 2013, while commemorating the tenth anniversary of UN Global Compact, the World Business Council of Sustainable Development, a chief executive officer (CEO)-led organization founded on the eve of the Rio Earth Summit in 1992, also joined UN Global Compact and GRI to strengthen the movement. The three organizations are combining their resources to enable businesses to become more responsible to society.

On 6 July 2011, the UN General Assembly adopted the 'Guiding Principles on Business and Human Rights: Implementing the United Nations "Protect, Respect, and Remedy" Framework' (the UN Framework), a report by Harvard Law School professor and UN Special Representative John Ruggie. As per the UN Framework, governments must clearly spell out their policies to protect human rights and communicate these to business organizations. Further, businesses must undertake regular human rights impact assessments (HRIA) and due diligence, and create internal policies to ensure compliance with human rights norms.

In fact, the concepts developed by these initiatives must be implemented for corporations to become trustees of society's wealth, rather than being just a slogan. Hopefully, more leaders will have the courage to break out of the pressure from their peers to comply with prevalent norms. They will lead the rest higher up the ladder of business responsibility.

SCORECARDS OF NATIONS: MIS-MEASURING OUR LIVES

Governments and business corporations are two principal institutions that impact the course of citizens' daily lives. On one hand, corporations provide us with many products and services, adding new innovations, without which we could not have the high standards of living that people in the developed world enjoy and to which people in developing countries aspire. Governments provide citizens with services in areas such as health, education and public transport which are also essential to our daily lives. Governments also provide many public services, such as the police and courts, without which we could not live securely.

Sadly, the level of citizens' trust in institutions of both business and government has been declining globally, according to the 2013 edition of the Edelman Trust Barometer, a global survey of trust in business and government institutions. It reports that only 19 per cent of those surveyed trusted business leaders to make ethical and moral decisions, and 18 per cent trusted that business leaders told the truth. The numbers for government leaders were even lower: 14 per cent and 13 per cent respectively.

The two decades between the fall of the Berlin Wall (which marked the 'end of history' and triumph of liberal capitalism according to Fukuyama) and the onset of the global financial crisis with the collapse of Lehman Brothers in 2008 were the go-go days of capitalism. In those heady days, the world's business and government leaders congregated annually at the World Economic Forum's meetings in the Swiss resort of Davos. There they celebrated the success of the global capitalist enterprise and discussed their solutions to the world's problems.

It was often pointed out that the revenues of some multinational corporations (MNCs) exceeded the budgets of many governments. Heads of elected governments came to Davos where CEOs lectured them on how governments must do more to free businesses from government shackles. It was suggested that governments should be run with the efficiency of large corporations, and heads of developing countries' governments were exhorted to emulate CEOs. In those days it became a compliment for a head of a government to be described as a CEO by business leaders.

In those years of corporate triumphalism, Lee Kuan Yew, former prime minister of Singapore, who had created a very successful corporate state, visited India in 2006. He met Narayana Murthy, founder of Infosys, the remarkably successful Indian information technology (IT) company, greatly admired for its high standards of corporate governance. In a public meeting they discussed 'governance', a subject both were most interested in and which, they felt, was the key to improving India's economic performance. Lee suggested that Murthy should take a more active role in the governance of India, to which the latter replied humbly that he was not equipped for the job. He said a business enterprise was primarily concerned with the efficient use of resources and production of economic surpluses, whereas a leader of a democratic institution has to also be deeply concerned with social and political outcomes. The more difficult problem of leadership in a democracy, he suggested, is managing 'equity' (not the shareholder variety) rather than 'efficiency'.

Murthy makes a very good point. Large countries, and especially those with competitive political parties and democratically elected governments, cannot be compared with large business corporations—even those whose revenues may equal countries' GDPs. The two institutions are structurally different and require different competencies to govern them. Having advised CEOs and executives of large companies in many parts of the world for twenty years and then, for five years, seeing the challenges of governing a large, federal, democratic country from the cockpit of India's Planning Commission, I can vouch for this.

Leaders in government have more complex missions to accomplish than corporate CEOs. A critical difference is in the source of the authority of leaders in government, especially democratic governments. Corporate leaders are appointed from above—by their boards; many also obtain power from their personal, large shareholdings. On the other hand, leaders in democratic governments must obtain their authority from the people they have to lead. Therefore, they cannot impose their writ on people in the same way that a corporate leader may on employees in the corporation. In public management, the people also have the power to hire and fire their leaders.

Another significant difference is the difficulty in defining what the value to be created is and for whom. In the corporate sector, 'value' can be simply, though too narrowly, defined as value for the shareholders of the enterprise. This can be measured in monetary terms. Leaders in democratic governments must negotiate goals and missions with the public. An agreement with the people, who are the ones to elect government leaders, about what exactly they value is not easy to obtain. Government leaders must consult widely to obtain consensus on goals, and define measures even for intangible goals.

Nicolas Sarkozy, while serving as president of France, constituted a commission in 2009. The task of this Ccommission was to examine systems of measurement of the economic performance and the social progress of nations. He asked three widely respected economists, Nobel laureates Joseph E. Stieglitz and Amartya Sen and the French economist Jean-Paul Fitoussi, to examine what a new scorecard of the progress of nations should be. The three economists produced a report they titled *Mismeasuring our Lives: Why GDP Doesn't Add up* (2010).

Sarkozy says in the foreword:

> We have built a cult of the data, and we are now enclosed within. The enormous consequences of what we have done are beginning to dawn on us…..Our statistics and accounts reflect our aspirations, the values that we assign things. They are inseparable from our vision of the world and the economy, of society, and our conception of human beings and our relations…With all this in mind, I asked Joseph Stieglitz, Amartya Sen, and Jean-Paul Fitoussi to set up a commission…To remedy the situation we face, we had to break out of old ways of thinking. A debate had to be launched at last.

I will not reproduce here all the recommendations of this seminal report by these eminent economists. I highlight only some of their insights.

They state in the preface to their report:

> We see the world through lenses not only shaped by our ideologies and ideas but also by the statistics we use

to measure what is going on, the latter being frequently linked to the former. GDP per capita is the commonly used metric; governments are pleased when they can report that GDP per capita has arisen, say by 5%. But other numbers can tell a very different picture.

'Well-being' and 'happiness', which many summarize as the outcome that citizens desire from progress, are multidimensional concepts. Examining the academic research and a number of concrete initiatives around the world (which include Bhutan's Gross National Happiness project) the commission has listed eight dimensions of 'well-being'. These are:

i. Material living standards (income, consumption and wealth)
ii. Health
iii. Education
iv. Personal activities including work
v. Political voice and governance
vi. Social connections and relationships
vii. Environment (present and future conditions)
viii. Insecurity of an economic as well as physical nature

Many of these dimensions are qualitative and instruments to measure them have not been developed yet. The list of dimensions may also change with further research. Better scorecards need to be developed because economists and policymakers attempting to guide the economy and society 'are like pilots trying to steer a course without a reliable compass', according to Stieglitz et al. (2010).

They also say (in the preface):

Metrics that seem out of synch with individuals' perceptions are particularly problematic. If GDP is increasing, but most people feel worse off, they may worry that governments are manipulating the statistics, in the hope that by telling them that they are better off, they will feel better off. In these cases, confidence in government is eroded, and with this confidence, the ability of government to address issues of vital public importance is eroded.

Let us apply these ideas about measurement to examine how India may be doing. The scenarios of India presented in Chapter 2 showed that India's citizens were rapidly losing faith in institutions of government. India's GDP was growing, and the Planning Commission publicly declared that poverty had reduced a lot. Citizens suspected something was amiss in these statistics because GDP growth and the poverty numbers reported by the Planning Commission did not reveal the reality they experienced in their lives.

India's goals of development, broadly accepted by all and expressed in the objectives of its 12th Five Year Plan, are faster, more inclusive and sustainable growth. These are also the goals of many other countries. Therefore, one can compare India's progress vis-à-vis other countries.

First, how well is India doing compared to the others? Many comparisons have been made by international agencies. Amongst the clearest is the Sustainable Economic Development (SEDA) framework recently developed by The Boston Consulting Group. SEDA is an instrument for assessing the effectiveness of countries in converting GDP growth to 'well-being' of their citizens. SEDA considers performance along ten dimensions as the indicators of overall well-being. These are GDP per capita, economic stability, infrastructure, employment, education, health, income inequality, governance, civil society, and impact on the environment. SEDA co-relates growth in GDP per capita with the other variables to determine a coefficient of transformation of GDP wealth into overall well-being in the country.

SEDA compares the relationship between levels of wealth and well-being of all countries in the most recent year for which Boston Consulting Group had the data, which was 2011 for most countries. It also includes a comparison of the performance over the previous five years: how was growth in wealth in these years converting into well-being? The combination of these two measures provides an evaluation of the 'policy matrix' of the country's growth strategy, that is, how is improvement on all dimensions being managed along with growth. Since India's goals are faster, more inclusive and more sustainable growth, the SEDA analysis is very relevant.

How India fares in converting increase in GDP (which was high in the years studied by Boston Consulting) to well-being can be assessed by comparing India's performance with its peers. Boston Consulting has chosen twelve countries as India's peers. These are the three other BRICs countries, five countries in Southeast Asia including Indonesia and the Philippines, and our four neighbours—Pakistan, Bangladesh, Sri Lanka, and Nepal. What this reveals is that India seems to be doing worse than its peers, and even worse than its neighbours.

The two dimensions along which India fares worst are generation of employment and protection of the environment while growing its GDP. The country ranks relatively high, in terms of its present position, with respect to governance and economic stability. But its performance on both these dimensions is assessed as having deteriorated in recent years—an evaluation that Indian citizens would agree with.

What can India learn from other countries about how to improve its performance? The Bertelsmann Foundation of Germany has done a study of 'Winning Strategies for a Sustainable

Future'. Bertelsmann studied thirty-five countries around the world that appear to be leaders in developing strategies for sustainable growth. Bertelsmann examined the quality of their strategies, the frameworks for implementation, and results so far. Then the list was narrowed to five countries for deeper study. From the study of these thirty-five countries, and further insights from the five, Bertelsmann selected five key success factors. Two of these must be highlighted because they are the starting points of the process of faster improvement.

The first is that sustainability policy derives from an overriding concept and guiding principles that are made to permeate significant areas of politics and society. And 'best practice' to make this happen is to get specific in national debates about a new scorecard of progress. Effective scorecards are not merely lists of measures cobbled together. They have an overarching concept to integrate measures of growth, social impact and environmental sustainability.

The second requirement for success is that a sustainability policy must be developed and implemented in a participatory manner. Therefore, the task for countries is to develop new participatory formats. Not only must large numbers of people be engaged, but different constituents must listen to each other too. The country must have an integrative vision of its future to unite it and a balanced scorecard to guide it. The task, to be taken up by whosoever political leaders and policymakers will lead their country, is to lead and facilitate this dialogue amongst the citizens of their country.

BALANCED SCORECARDS

Nations and even business corporations are complex systems with many subsystems that interact with each other. The condition of all critical subsystems must be gauged to know the health of the whole system.

The term often used to describe the new scorecards being used by some corporations to measure their performance is 'balanced'. Measurements are made in three or four domains: economic, environmental, social, and governance. It is very tempting to convert these three or four into a single measure. This would make it easy to compare and rank companies. But valuable information required to manage the companies would be lost.

Consider an aeroplane. It is a complex system with many subsystems. A pilot must have many gauges in the cockpit and monitor several variables to fly an aeroplane safely. Amongst these are the speed and the altitude of the aeroplane. Providing the pilot with only one gauge displaying a combination measure of speed and altitude would be very dangerous for the pilot and passengers aboard. If the plane is flying dangerously low, albeit at a very high speed, the gauge would report an aggregated good performance. The pilot would not know he is flying into danger.

Adding many independent variables into a single number requires relative weights to be given to each of them. How shall weights be assigned to independent variables? The hazards in assigning weights are illustrated by the difficulty the US Air Force has been having for many years in selecting a replacement for its ageing fleet of refuelling tankers. The selection process has been stalled several times by ethics scandals and legal challenges by losers whenever the US Air Force announced its decision. Therefore, the authorities decided to remove all subjective elements in the evaluation. A total of 373 mandatory requirements have been laid out, each of which must be met on a simple pass-fail basis. In this effort, to avoid any bias in the weighting, the water flow in toilets is rated as highly as the fuel offload rate!

These examples illustrate the need for the designer of the

instrument panel to understand the structure of the system that is being monitored. What are the critical subsystems that enable it to function? For gauging the health of our bodies, we should know how all our vital systems are functioning. Compare two persons. One has a very strong liver and a very weak heart. Another has an adequately functioning liver along with an adequately functioning heart. Whose life is in greater danger? If the conditions of heart and liver were added into one number, both would be the same, whereas in fact one person is clearly in greater danger.

Another reason why a single measure is dangerous is that both flows as well as stocks in a system must be measured and monitored separately. Good corporate managers know that while increasing 'flows' by pursuing growth of production and sales numbers, they should keep an eye on their balance sheet—the 'stock' of capital. Indeed, the collapse of most dot-com companies during the boom in the late 1990s was due to the failure to observe this simple principle.

Stieglitz et al. (2010) explain why, in the management of economies of countries, measures of stock and flows must be maintained separately. GDP is a measure of flow—of production and consumption activity in a country, and in the world. The more we consume our stock of natural resources, the more the GDP increases. The excessive attention to the measurement of GDP, which is an aggregated measure of flow, has vicious effects. Damage to the environment reduces the stock of natural capital while it may increase economic activity.

For example, the BP oil spill in the Gulf of Mexico set off expenditures of billions of dollars of legal fees and clean-up costs. These have added to the US' GDP. Thus BPs carelessness and the oil spill contributed to a large increase in US' GDP at a time when the country's reeling economy needed a boost. If we only cared about GDP growth we should celebrate! However, we sense that we must care for our natural environment too. Therefore, a single picture of a brown pelican whose wings were immobilized by gooey crude oil could evoke such great outrage against BP.

If we do not mind the stock of our natural capital, we can go bankrupt by running out of our natural resources—or natural 'capital'—which is what environmentalists have been warning us about. Nations have social capital too. Large components of this social capital are citizens' trust in institutions and the quality of relationships in communities. When trust in institutions runs too low, the flows of economic activities can run low too. This is perhaps the root cause of India's declining GDP in recent years.

7

DEMOCRACY AND DIVISIONS

Democracy allies itself with change and proceeds from the assumption that nobody knows enough, that nothing is final, and that the old order (whether of men or institutions) will be dragged offstage when its prescriptions no longer fit the facts.

—Lewis H. Lapham

STRUCTURES FOR DEMOCRACY

Democracies like houses need structures and systems to function. A house needs walls to divide space into rooms. It also needs systems for ventilation, electricity supply and plumbing. However, structures and systems alone are not enough to transform a house into a functioning home for its occupants. A happy home is made so by the practices and habits of those who live in it. Therefore, it should not be surprising that a happy, functioning family and an unhappy, dysfunctional family could be living in identical houses: because while they may live within identical houses, the pattern and quality of their interactions could be very different.

No doubt the architecture of the house can influence the pattern of interaction of its residents. Though all houses may have some common rooms, such as a living room in which people could come together, one house could have many private rooms which people can maintain according to their own tastes, whereas another could have fewer, larger rooms that require people to negotiate the use of those rooms with each other. But whatever be the arrangement of the walls and rooms, it is the quality of their relationships, and the respect they have for each other, that distinguish happy homes from unhappy ones.

Structures in democracy delineate the roles of the legislature, the judiciary and the executive. They also divide authority and responsibility amongst the centre, the states and local bodies. The number of political parties is another dimension of structure. Like a house, democracy requires structures and systems for it to function. Like in a good home, patterns of interactions should also be established for people to listen to each other, appreciate each other, and live happily together.

The principle of majority rule—that the will of the majority, determined by voting, should prevail—is a central tenet in democracies. However, a problem with this principle is that minorities can be unreasonably subjugated, even tyrannized, by laws 'democratically' framed by the majority. The Sunnis in Iraq found themselves in a corner when the Shia majority elected a government. A more egregious example is Adolf Hitler and the Nazi Party in Germany. Elected by a majority of German citizens, Hitler and the Nazis viciously persecuted a minority—the Jewish citizens. Examples such as these suggest that elections and votes should not be the only or even the principal operative structures on which democracy depends. Democracies must have other structures and processes to include all people and ensure they are justly treated. Law courts are one such structure. But courts are enjoined to interpret and apply laws, and not create their own laws. Since the laws are created by the principle of majority rule, the judiciary cannot be a remedy for the structural limitation of a democracy that is overly dependent on this principle.

Examining structures of democracies in thirty-six countries, Arend Lijphart analyses two basic patterns of democracies in his book, *Patterns of Democracy: Government Forms and Performance in Thirty-Six Countries* (1999). One is 'majoritarian' and the other is 'consensual'. In majoritarian democracies, majority rule is the norm. (Generally there are two principal parties in such democracies, but there could be more.) The party that gets the most votes rules and the power to govern is then concentrated in this party. The losers must oppose. The tyranny of the majority is expected to be mitigated by the rotation of the party in power over time. On the other hand, in consensual democracies power is spread across more organs of the state and perhaps amongst more political parties too. Britain, according to Lijphart, is the most majoritarian of the thirty-six democracies he has studied and Switzerland the most consensual.

One would expect that consensual democracies, as analysed by Lijphart, where power is more devolved and there are more political parties, would be slower to arrive at agreements and would hence be less efficient. For example, Switzerland has three official languages and is divided into many independent cantons. The Swiss must work harder to ensure that the solutions work for all compared to people in democracies like Britain which is united by one language and has much less devolution of powers. Therefore, Lipjhart's analysis that consensual democracies generally perform better than majoritarian democracies is pleasantly surprising.

There may be two explanations for this. One is that the measures of performance Lijphart uses include many social measures, such as health, education, crime, care of the elderly, and care of the environment, in addition to economic growth. Consensual democracies have 'kinder, gentler qualities', he says. The other explanation could be that majoritarian democracies breed dissent: losers make it their business to make life difficult for the winners. With weaker processes for arriving at consensus, differences are more difficult to resolve in majoritarian democracies. Thus decision-making stalls when collaboration is required between the governing party and the opposition.

CONSENSUAL DEMOCRACY

With this analysis, some assertions may now be made about the structures and processes required for a healthy democracy. First, a popular view of democracy—that it is principally a system of fair (and frequent) elections to determine the will of the majority—which was projected in television pictures of people lining up at polling booths in Afghanistan, Iraq and other such newly 'democratized' countries in President George W. Bush's campaign to spread democracy through the world is a dangerously facile view. Second, to remain healthy, democracies will require more devolution, and the participation of many more people in democratic institutions, to counter the pressures from the erosion of national institutions on one hand and the rise of liberal, individualistic values on the other. Therefore, many more people will have to participate in deliberations, in many forums, to democratically determine policies that affect their lives. This leads to the conclusion that the quality of their deliberations and their respect for others' views, and not the fairness of elections, may be the key to effective democracy.

Democracy's formal structures, such as constitutions and electoral systems, are important for a democracy to function smoothly. Elections provide for upward representation. They are the vertical threads—the warp of democracy's fabric. Institutional processes for dialogue amongst citizens laterally are democracy's weft. It is the quality of the dialogue and deliberations amongst citizens that strengthens the fabric of democracy.

Consensual democracies require agreements about the means and goals of development. Often ideological and deep conceptual divisions about the goals and means of progress make it difficult to obtain consensus. I will highlight five such divisions.

INDIVIDUALS OR COMMUNITIES?

On one side of the first division is the ideal of individual freedom and free markets. The belief in the supremacy of the rights of individuals can run deep. The ideal of the rights of the individual is described as 'self-evident' in the US Constitution. The growth of the US to become the predominant country in the world, which it is today, is often ascribed to the determined application in its internal politics, society and economy of the principle of supremacy of individual rights. As a contrast, the Soviet Union's decay, and by extension the weakness of communism as an ideology, is attributed to its application of the opposite principle, that of the power of all-pervasive government. The fall of the Soviet Empire marked the 'end of history' of ideological conflict, with the final victory of the ideology of individual freedom, according to Francis Fukuyama's famous essay.

However, the ideological conflict between the supremacy of individual rights versus the rights of the community (with government as the community's agent) has not ended, according to an influential, right-wing group that has been campaigning to change the composition of the US Supreme Court to support its agenda. This group, a forerunner of the Tea Party, refers to its cause as the 'Constitution in Exile'. It believes that the cardinal constitutional principle, of supremacy of the rights of the individual, was eroded by Roosevelt's New Deal which began the movement for a stronger role for government. The New Deal was Roosevelt's and the US Democratic Party's solution to protect the weaker sections of society from the effects of unregulated competition and markets that had led to the depression in the US economy between the two world wars. This right-wing group would like the Supreme Court to strike down regulations such as the Federal Communications Commission, the Environmental Protection Agency, and perhaps even the Securities and Exchange Commission as unconstitutional.

The Constitution in Exile movement is extreme in its view, carrying too far a principle that pervades free market ideas: the rights and rewards of individuals. This principle plays out in many ways in the constructs of distributive systems in societies and incentive systems in business organizations. But this principle can be taken too far, with deleterious effects on cooperation within organizations as well as societies.

The difference of earnings within business organizations has increased steeply as free market ideologies have gained strength. In the 1970s, the difference between the average earnings of chief executive officers (CEOs) and median earnings of others in US organizations was 25:1. This increased to 100:1 by 1990 and is reported to have increased even further to 250:1 by 2010. In India, where free market ideologies came into force only in the early 1990s, the increase in disparities has been much steeper. The difference in earnings between CEOs and the median earnings of employees remained at around 25:1 from the 1970s till the 1990s (all the years I worked in a senior position with the Tata Group in India, as mentioned earlier). By 2010, the disparity in India had also increased to 250:1.

Such disparities are sought to be justified by the exceptional contribution that CEOs supposedly make to the performance of their organizations as compared to the contributions of all others in the organization. The differences in the ways CEOs and others have contributed to their organizations—how hard they have worked and how smart they are—could not have changed by as much as ten times within fifteen years in India (or over thirty years in the US). No, the increase in the differentials can only be explained by changes in norms within organizations and societies.

On the other side of this ideological divide is the ideal of a harmonious community, with rules and institutions of governance that guide and restrain the behaviour of its individual members. Individuals, communities and nations desire harmony in the world around themselves primarily because it gives them security. One can walk more freely in the streets of a city that is free of crime. Corporations can trade more securely and people can travel more safely when nations are not at war. Second, cooperation in caring for the 'commons' can also make the world more pleasant: for example, clean cities are more pleasant to walk in. And, third, observation of common rules also increases the ability of people to engage with each other, through trade, telecommunications, the Internet, etc.

However, harmony and high quality 'commons' come at a price to individual freedom. People have to observe rules and behaviour that damages the commons cannot be permitted. Such restraints on individual freedom bother ideological extremists, like the Constitution in Exile group. They would not have any external authority curb the freedom of the individual. And a similar fear at the back of their minds (even though they may not have such extreme views) explains the apprehensions of many US leaders towards systems of global governance in international relations. They do not want the US government's right to determine what is in its best interest to be constrained by a global institution. In fact, the more democratic that institution is by giving equal votes to all countries rich or poor, the greater the apprehension in the US (and some other rich countries) that the poor will have a majority and take decisions that will hurt the rich countries. Thus the creation of a global governance system, which is a means to create a safer and better world, which US leaders say is the goal of their international policies, is being prevented by their own ideological and deep-seated fears.

TRANSACTIONS OR TRUST?

One of the strongest ideologies in the world today is the faith in the efficiency of free markets. According to a school of economists and policymakers, who have been powerful since the 1990s, free markets are the solution to the economic development of the world and all countries in it. Their case is built on the logic of economic efficiency of free markets that should enable the most efficient producers of any product or service to emerge. Thus, in their model, all economic activities, through some efficient process of competition, will be performed by the most efficient entities which will then trade with each other what each does best. Thereby, according to this school, the world will use its overall resources most efficiently for the benefit of all mankind.

Trade between people involves transactions. Therefore, transaction costs between the various actors in the economy must be reduced to create efficient markets. Many economists have emphasized the importance of 'trust' within societies to reduce transaction costs and enhance economic progress; which is why they are interested in the conditions that create trust amongst people. The principal conditions for creating trust, according to economists, are: (*i*) availability of adequate and symmetrical information to the parties involved; and (*ii*) confidence that all parties will comply with their obligations in the transaction. Therefore, in free market economies it is necessary to have institutions such as stock market regulators that are empowered to ensure transparency and adequacy of information, and ensure compliance with rules, to ensure that the market continues to function with low transaction costs.

The transactional mode of working with others, if properly governed by written, or widely accepted 'unwritten rules', creates confidence in the predictability of actions of the parties involved. Hence it is efficient—in economic terms—and also adds to the stock of 'trust' in society. But this trust is limited to the bounds of the transactions, and does not automatically extend beyond them. To put it simply, it may be observed that New Yorkers know how to complete daily transactions with each other quickly and efficiently, with no waste of time on pleasantries. But New Yorkers are also known for avoiding needless contact with strangers because their instinct is not to trust them.

It is necessary to distinguish different types of situations in which trust is required. One type, already explained, is 'market transactions' between strangers. In such situations, the actors trust that *the system* will ensure that others will perform to their contracts within the context of that system. They will not necessarily trust these others outside the purview of that system, as the example of the New Yorkers illustrates, because they cannot predict how they will act in a different context. An established system provides the scaffolding for working safely within its contained space. Therefore, what we must examine is what will engender trust between parties interacting in situations beyond the safety of accepted systems, or when the rules governing the system have to be substantially changed—in other words, when there is no scaffolding, or the scaffolding has to be realigned with the parties working inside.

In such situations a deeper trust is required in *each other*, and not merely trust in the system. For this there must be confidence that the other is unlikely to cause harm. Therefore, the parties must know the principles that will guide the other's actions, and know each other's wants and fears. They can learn these through the hit-and-miss of trying to work with each other, which could lead to greater mistrust. Or they can sit down and listen to each other's aspirations and beliefs, and locate the tripwires they will watch out for and help each other across, and thus build stronger coalitions.

Such deep dialogues are not the norm when parties try to work together. Perhaps they should be, to build *trusting relationships*, create stronger partnerships, and strengthen the foundations for a richer and happier society.

GROSS NATIONAL PRODUCT OR GROSS NATIONAL HAPPINESS?

A process of change and development must have a goal. And agreement on the goal is necessary to create partnerships for development. But it is not easy to agree on the goal because there are ideological differences and conceptual challenges.

An article in *The New York Times* in April 2005 said that Norwegians have no business to feel rich when the 'facts' show they are not. According to this article, Norwegian consumers had fewer choices of goodies than people in New York and generally paid more for what they bought. Moreover, the average private consumption figure in the US was $32,900, whereas in Norway it was only $18,350. Even the public facilities in Norway are not in as good condition as those in the US. Therefore, according to this article, Norwegians are wrong to feel rich. But what irks the author of the article is that, nevertheless, they do!

The article is another pointer to the inadequacy of purely economic measures, such as growth of gross domestic product (GDP) per capita, as goals of national development policy. And another reminder that happiness is not obtained merely by making people richer. It raises the question, what should be the goals of the socio-economic development of a nation, if not increase of their GDP and per capita incomes? The Kingdom of Bhutan has chosen to pursue Gross National Happiness as its objective. Should this be the goal? The problem is that while we know how to measure the size of economies, we do not know how to measure happiness, and are not even certain about what makes people really happy. We must also understand the correlation between growth in national incomes and the happiness of people.

Which brings us to the million dollar question: what makes people happier if it is not a million dollars? The General Social Survey of the US reveals seven major factors. A person's financial situation is only one, and that too not the most important. The other six are: family relationships, community and friends, personal freedom, the nature of work the person is engaged in, health, and personal values. Therefore, a national development paradigm that puts GDP per capita as the most important measure of success cannot guarantee that people will be happier. Indeed, a development paradigm focused excessively on stimulating economic output per capita will, over time, destroy many principal sources of happiness. For example, while the greater willingness of people in the US, as compared to many European countries, to move to other places for better jobs may contribute to the US economy's dynamism and higher productivity, it also disrupts the stability and quality of family and community life. Thus it has a negative impact on two of the most important sources of happiness for people.

India has been striving to increase the growth of its GDP. It broke out of the 'Hindu rate' of growth of about 3 per cent in which it was mired until the economic reforms that commenced in the 1980s. By 2006, its growth rate was exceeding 8 per cent per annum. With a growth rate second only to China's, India could justly proclaim then that it was the world's fastest growing free market democracy. However, as India's government and business leaders contemplated how to accelerate GDP growth even more, some amongst them pointed out that a pattern of growth that does not address issues of equity and sustainability would not be desirable. Farmers who were unable to pay the loans they had taken to purchase fertilizers and seeds have committed suicide because the prices of their produce were inadequate. Tribal areas, ignored by the country's economic drive, are overrun by armed revolutionaries.

Pursuit of more GDP is a simplistic model of development. GDP and per capita incomes cannot be the measures of the development of society. A more holistic model is required that integrates the perspectives of the various social sciences. As Douglass C. North writes in *Understanding the Process of Economic Change* (2010: 11):

> The human environment is a human construct of rules, norms, conventions, and ways of doing things that define the framework of human interaction. This human environment is divided by social scientists into discrete disciplines—economics, political sciences, sociology—but the constructions of the human mind that we require to make sense of the human environment do not coincide with these artificial categories. Our analytical frameworks must integrate insights derived from these artificially separate disciplines if we are to understand the process of change.

The problem in combining the perspectives of the various social sciences is that their proponents do not know how to talk to each other. They have their own jargon, which is generally understood only within their own community. And they have their special models of the world, in which they include only those factors they consider important. Indeed, the proponents of the various social disciplines may not even *like* talking to each other. Not wanting to talk, nor able to talk with each other, they live within 'conceptually gated communities', only talking to and listening to their own kind.

CAPITALISM OR DEMOCRACY?

Posing capitalism and democracy in opposition may startle readers. Deep down, in the principles on which these two institutions are founded, they are indeed incompatible. Capitalist institutions run on the principle that one dollar equals one vote. Therefore, those who have more dollars to invest in an enterprise must have a larger say on how the enterprise is run. On the other hand, democracy says that every human being, rich or poor, has an equal vote. When systems that run on different principles connect, there will be dissonance. It is like connecting an appliance that runs on direct current (DC) into a socket with alternating (AC) current. Something will blow up.

Lester Thurow, former dean of the MIT Sloan School of Management, points out in *The Future of Capitalism: How Today's Economic Forces Shape Tomorrow's World* (1997: 242):

> Democracy and capitalism have very different beliefs about the proper distribution of power. One believes in a completely equal distribution of political power: one man, one vote, while the other believes that it is the duty of the economically fit to drive the unfit out of business and into economic extinction. "Survival of the fittest" and inequalities in purchasing power are what capitalist efficiency is all about.

In his book, *False Dawn: The Delusions of Global Capitalism*

(1998: 17), John Gray, conservative political thinker and former advisor to Margaret Thatcher, warns that 'Democracy and the free market are rivals, not allies.'

Capitalism and democracy have become ideologies. The US has led a crusade to spread both capitalism and democracy across the world. Francis Fukuyama, in his treatise *The End of History and the Last Man* (1992) said that the history of ideological conflict had ended in 1989 with the fall of the Soviet Union. Western ideas of free-market capitalism and electoral democracy had triumphed over state-run economies and totalitarian governments. It is ironic that the ideological conflicts that have emerged since 1989, with the arising of the more than perfect storm explained in Chapter 1, are between institutions of capitalism and democracy, the two supposed victors in Fukuyama's historical war.

The development of institutions that conform to both democratic principles as well as market-capitalist ideas may be human history's unfinished task.

Perhaps it has become modern India's destiny to finish the task. The Indian political landscape is churning. Parties of the left, right and centre are manoeuvring for elected space. 'While the West often tries to discuss the world in black and white terms, the Indian mind is able to see the world in many different colors,' says Kishore Mahbubani in *The New Asian Hemisphere: The Irresistible Shift of Global Power to the East* (2008). Therefore, I ask, 'Could India provide the bridge between free-market capitalism and democracy?'

This new order must meet two essential requirements. First, a just system must be based on the 'self-evident' principle the US founding fathers laid down, that all peoples are 'endowed by their creator with certain inalienable rights' even if they are not equally rich or equally powerful. This principle is the heart of the democratic ideal to take civilization to a higher order.

Second, this system must be founded on the principle that

business and the economy are not the be-all and end-all of life. Social and political aspirations are part of human reality too.

I was gifted a tie by a venerable capitalist journal in New York whose offices I visited with an Indian business delegation in 2003 when India's GDP was increasing rapidly and the country's government claimed that 'India was Shining'. Emblazoned on the tie, in gold, are the words, 'Capitalist Tool'. I have never worn the tie because, though I am OK with being called a capitalist, I am not OK with being anybody's tool! The challenge before us as we march into the 21st century is to make capitalism and economics our tools, rather than human beings becoming their tools. Therefore, let us first determine our aspirations and principles, and accordingly devise the form of capitalism and economics we want.

TO HAVE OR TO BE?

Stepping back to look at the pattern in these divides, a deeper chasm may be perceived. In his seminal book, *To Have or To Be?* (1978) psychologist-philosopher Erich Fromm describes the deep chasm between the 'having' and the 'being' modes of living.

Fromm describes the 'having' mode as an acquisitive mode, in which, he says, 'To acquire, to own, and to make a profit are the sacred and unalienable rights of the individual. What the sources of property are does not matter; nor does possession impose any obligations on the property owners' (p. 69).

This philosophy sounds eerily like the views of the Constitution in Exile group in the US (mentioned earlier). Step back a moment and we realize that the push to acquire is what is driving the growth of economies and our lives with it. When the US economy slumped, President George W. Bush famously declared that it was the patriotic duty of citizens to buy more. Advertisers make economies move. They push us to acquire more, to have what others have, and newer versions of what we already have. So we accumulate more stuff, and have to discard stuff too. Resource industries have to dig more stuff out of the ground—oil and ores—to feed the industrial-consumer machine. Then this machine must find more places to dispose the garbage it produces.

The 'being' mode is a search for happiness and well-being, and for meaning in one's life. Fromm's description of the being mode is a beautifully spiritual one, but it need not detain us further. To link Fromm's descriptions of the having and being modes to our analysis of the prevalent norms of societal and business institutions, it is sufficient to recall Hirschman's analysis of the relationship of corporations and people. Business corporations see people only as customers, he said. They do not know how to communicate with them as citizens, and perhaps do not want to. Corporations want a 'share of wallet', not a share of heart. A share of the citizen's heart has no utility for them if it does not make the citizen open her wallet.

Fromm proposes the having and being modes as an 'either-or' proposition. I fear it is not so simple. There are many people in the world, millions of whom are in my country, who need to have more, just to have the basic needs and dignities of life—enough food to eat, sufficient clothes to wear, and a roof over their heads.

Richard Layard, while making his case for happiness in his book, *Happiness: Lessons from a New Science* (2005), confirms that people in very poor countries are less happy than people in the richest countries. After all, extra income is really valuable when it lifts people out of sheer poverty by enabling them to buy adequate food and shelter, which are the most basic requirements in Maslow's hierarchy of needs. Therefore, it is imperative to raise income levels in poor countries such as India.

Layard also points out that while incomes per head have almost tripled in the US, as a result of the remarkable growth of its economy since 1945, the percentage of poor people in the US who say they are very happy has remained the same, at less than 30 per cent. His explanation is that they yearn for better quality relationships and more meaning in their lives. So we must conclude that for happiness having and being cannot be a pursuit of 'either-or'. It must be a search for 'both-and'. The word 'balance' comes to mind again.

QUANTITIES AND QUALITIES

The five divisions I have framed are:

- A. Individuals or Communities?
- B. Transactions or Trust?
- C. Gross National Product or Gross National Happiness?
- D. Capitalism or Democracy?
- E. To Have or To Be?

What one 'has' one can weigh, count and measure. What one 'is', is hard to define and measure. Looking down the list of the divides one may hear the language of quantities more loudly in the left side of each division, and the language of qualities on the right side. It is much easier to construct scorecards for what is on the left—product, capital and what one has. It is not easy to put numbers to trust, happiness and what one is. Though it is not easy to measure the quality of a community, or the happiness of a person, or their self-respect and dignity, we have seen that these are qualities that everyone aspires for.

'Balanced' scorecards must include both the left and right sides; our necessities as well as our aspirations. The redirection of the progress of the world, which has become imperative to avoid the looming risks of environmental degradation and the sociopolitical risks due to the perceptions of increasing inequities, must begin with a new definition of success founded on a new aspirational vision. Visions cannot be conveyed only in numbers. Perhaps they need no numbers. Visions express 'what' we want, even if we do not know how to measure it.

Economists at the Global Economic Symposium in Kiel on 'Redefining Success' (mentioned earlier), insisted that we need measurements because one can manage only what can be measured. Yet, at the conclusion of the symposium, an economist admitted that what he wanted most of all is a world in which everyone has dignity, a quality not easy to define and very hard to put a number to.

BEING AND BECOMING

Great visions also suggest 'how' we may get what we want. Means and ends are not separable in great visions. A good life is always lived in the present, as philosophers including Erich Fromm keep reminding us. It is easy to describe a great future. It is much more difficult to develop a way to reach this great future without compromising what we value. Therefore any vision of a society whose means condone (or require) injustice and cruelty to citizens in the present as a sacrifice to create a great nation in the future cannot be a vision of a good society.

The values we will live by must not be separated from the value we seek to create in our institutions and societies. The pursuit of shareholder value, as the ultimate measure of corporate success since the 1990s, driven by the ideology that creation of shareholder wealth must be the purpose of business corporations, resulted in many bad practices. The means for producing shareholder value were secondary, or did not even matter to some executives, so long as their companies could appear on top of the lists of business magazines, as the greatest 'wealth creators', with wealth defined only as shareholder value.

Humanity is searching for designs of better institutions. The quality of institutions is not easy to measure. This is the economic modeller's dilemma. Explanations of the progress of nations are incomplete without an account of their institutions. The scenarios of India, explained in an earlier chapter, revealed the centrality of institutions to India's progress. In fact, the scenarios showed why a failure to reform the country's institutions since the 1990s, while making economic reforms, resulted in a deterioration of governance. The scenarios predicted a rapid decline in India's GDP growth which the country's economists had not predicted and its policymakers were not prepared for because in their models institutions were a non-quantifiable and hence exogenous variable. The quality of institutions and the pace of implementation of policies and projects are key determinants of the 'Total Factor Productivity' of an economy. The National Council of Applied Economic Research (NCAER), the Indian think tank that assisted the scenarists to estimate future growth rates, has undertaken the conceptual challenge of finding a method to include the condition of institutions and the ability to implement change in models of the Indian economy.

Great institutions, in business, non-governmental organizations (NGOs), governments, academia, and even political parties, are those whose members' conduct is guided by good values. Indeed, the great value they produce for society are the models of 'being', and the values they live by, that they provide for others to aspire to and emulate.

Aspirations are higher in the hierarchy of human wants than material and quantifiable needs. The yearning for a better world, which one cannot yet fully describe, is the force that causes transformational change to happen. When organizations and societies convert their shared aspirations to visions, they create a magnetic vision that draws them towards it.

8

CONSENSUS AND TRUST

There are always three sides to every story: your side, the other side, and the truth.

—ANONYMOUS

Visions cannot be painted with numbers alone. Visions may need no numbers. Visions express what we want in our lives, and the lives of our children and grandchildren, even if we do not know how to measure what we want. The shaping of shared visions requires a new dialogue.

Deliberations in which old arguments are rehashed; discussions in which both sides hold onto their positions; debates in which the objective is to prove the other side wrong will not produce agreements. 'Rally the troops, take the hill, or die on it' are the words of a Republican congressman to describe how his party was approaching negotiations with the Democrats just two days before the United States (US) government was in danger of defaulting on its debt in October 2013. This is not an approach likely to produce lasting agreements. This is the language of war.

The Navajo Indians in the US believe that if one ends a dispute with a winner and a loser, one dispute may have ended but another surely will have started because harmony will not have been restored.

Reforms cannot happen if everyone holds onto their positions.

The essence of democracy, deep down, is that all points of view are respected. The reform of institutions requires the reforming of written and unwritten rules. Therefore, reforms often challenge deeply held beliefs. They require changing the way we think.

REDESIGNING THE AEROPLANE WHILE FLYING

How we live is how we are. Our becoming is our being. Our means and our ends cannot be separated. These profound truths explain the essence of the process of institutional reform. Institutions are the vehicles in which societies travel and progress. We cannot get outside our institutions and change them from the outside. We have to change them from within as we travel in them.

Change is a process of letting go of some beliefs and habits, and adopting new beliefs and habits. Like a trapeze artist, or Tarzan in the jungle, we let go of one swing when we see another that can take us where we want to go. This is risky, but necessary if we want to progress.

Inertia is a law of physics. Systems resist change and so do people. They are afraid to let go of what they have: their power, their positions in hierarchies, their sources of income, or the places in which they live. Often they must: to enable change to be brought about. Processes of social, economic and institutional change create winners and losers, or at least perceptions of winners and losers. Losers will resist, and indeed they must, for it is the law of inertia. It is the instinct of preservation.

A mark of good democracies and great societies is that nobody's life is trampled on for the larger good. Minorities, even of one, must be cared for. Therefore, democracies need consensus for making change happen. The concerns of potential losers must be understood by those who hope to gain from the change. Adjustments must be made. No one should feel that they have been asked to leave their trapeze swing without another to hold.

In democracies, consensus is necessary for change. Failure to achieve consensus will stall change. This is considered as the weakness of democracies in the race for growth in gross domestic product (GDP). This is the excuse made for India when its growth rate is compared with China's.

In democracies, citizens must have the opportunities to speak in their own voices, unclear as they may sound to others. And it is this freedom to speak that creates the impression that there is greater discord within democracies than in those societies in which such freedoms are not given. Because discord cannot be suppressed in democracies, people in democratic societies need skills for consensus building to a greater extent than people living and working in non-democratic societies and institutions.

TAKING DECISIONS DEMOCRATICALLY

From my study window I looked down on the lawn of the condominium complex in which I lived. Every few months a meeting of the residents association would be called on this lawn. I would see the chairman struggling to create order while allowing people to speak. Finally, he would call the meeting to take a decision. His patience having run out, he would say, 'We have heard several useful views. I think we are all in agreement that....' He would then state the decision he had in mind and close the meeting.

I knew that the decision would not stick and the subject would come up again in the next meeting. I knew because this subject had been discussed in a previous meeting that I had also observed In that meeting, a previous chairman had similarly concluded the meeting by announcing his decision. That decision had been criticized by the residents when they had met later in their homes and on their evening walks. They had lost confidence in the chairman. Elections had been called and now it was a new chairman who was also struggling to arrive at a consensual decision on the same subject.

I have observed the same pattern of meetings after meetings to try and arrive at a decision that will stick at the highest levels of government too. Chairmen and participants of meetings are short of time. Many people are invited to speak, perhaps even everybody. But they do not listen to each other. The chairman concludes that all that was needed to be said has been said. He must show he is in charge and so, like the chairmen of the residents' welfare associations, he declares that there is a consensus and pronounces his decision. After the meeting it becomes evident that was no real consensus. The matter must be discussed again and another meeting will have to be called,

Reflecting on the failures of these chairmen, I recall how Nani Palkhivala, one of India's most brilliant lawyers and widely respected champions of democracy and human rights and chairman of several large corporations, conducted shareholders' meetings. Like most chairmen, he too, after allowing shareholders to speak, would call a vote and then quickly announce that the resolution proposed by management had been carried. And it always was. Though he seemed as arbitrary as the chairmen of the residents' associations, the shareholders did not lose confidence in him.

Why were the outcomes in the two situations—the residents' and shareholders' meetings—so different even though they seemed to follow the same procedure for decision making? To understand this, we must analyse how to align the process of decision making with the nature of issues being considered and the structures of the institutions within which the decisions are to be taken.

Decision-making modes can be classified into five types:

1. Minority rule: When one person, or some minority of persons, is given powers by the majority to take decisions on their behalf.

2. Majority rule: The most commonly used mode in a democracy whereby the will of the majority prevails even when the minority may strongly oppose it.
3. Consensus: When a minority may not have a high commitment to the course of action the majority is committed to but is, nevertheless, willing to go along with it.
4. Unanimity: When all have high commitment to the course of action.
5. 'Plop': When the commitment to the course of action has not been tested and a wrong assumption is made that there is adequate support

Minority Rule

When one person (or some minority of persons) is given powers by the majority to take certain decisions on their behalf, it is feasible for that person or minority to take decisions without the support of the majority present in a meeting. These authorized persons may consult their constituents if they wish even though they have the power to simply declare a decision that they have been empowered to take. Nani Palkhiwala, and other corporate chairmen, may politely listen to dissent from a majority present at a shareholders' meeting and go ahead with their decision ignoring opposition because they have been given sufficient proxies, legitimately obtained beforehand. The shareholders in the meeting know this. This is a situation in which 'minority rule' can work in the meeting. However, the chairmen of the residents' associations, not having similar powers given to them by due process beforehand, should not use this mode of decision making. They must choose one of the other modes.

Majority Rule

This is the most commonly used mode of decision making in a democracy. In fact, it is sometimes assumed that this is all there is to democracy: set up voting systems and let majorities prevail. The process is deceptively simple: ask people to make a choice against a proposition presented to them, preferably in a simple yes/no (or either/or) manner; count the votes for and against; determine whether the proposition was carried (or who won or lost).

Two problems muddy this seemingly straightforward process. One problem is that it is not easy to present every decision in a straightforward yes/no or either/or mode: often there are multiple choices. When there are several choices, the one that gets more votes than any of the others may be in an overall minority. All the losers may be closer to each other than to the winner. They may have lost because they were fragmented by the manner in which the options were framed. Such situations often create problems in electoral politics and can even result in tyrannies of minorities over majorities.

The second problem with this 'let us put it to vote' method is that propositions must be understood by the voters before they vote, even when it is a simple yes/no proposition. Otherwise, though it may seem that the proposition had support, there will be problems during implementation when what was implied becomes clearer.

Both these problems in making choices arise from the way the options are framed and presented. They can be overcome by clarifying what the options are beforehand through wider consultations with the voters. These consultations may suggest better ways to frame the options in terms that the voters will understand when they finally vote. Wider discussions before the vote can also clarify the issues to the voters, and can enable the problem and solutions proposed to be expressed in images and a language that they will understand.

Consensus

Democracy in America, as elsewhere, is based on the principles that all persons have inalienable rights and that every person, rich or poor, educated or not, has an equal vote. The thought that, with these principles, majorities may democratically deprive minorities of their wealth and their power often frightens some people who profess to be champions of democracy.

Whenever a powerful minority feels threatened by the power that the principle of 'one person one vote' gives to the majority in a democracy, it can suspend democratic principles. The United Nations (UN) Security Council is one such example, wherein a group of powerful nations, a minority within the community of nations, have chosen to keep certain powers to themselves. Moreover, within the council some nations have a power of veto, whereby whenever they dislike the outcome of a vote of members they can overrule it! Another example of a person in power suspending democracy when its outcomes seemed to hurt her interests was Indira Gandhi's suspension of democracy in India.

What if the minority in numbers is weak and does not have the power to over-rule the majority? For many decisions, a determination of what the majority wants is appropriate. A simplistic view of democracy requires that the minority must accept what the majority wants. However, there are some situations in which the imposition of the will of the majority on the minority would be wrong. For example, if the consequence of the decision is that the minority will be disenfranchised or subjugated by the majority, then democratic societies must not allow it. Therefore, voting to determine the will of the majority may not be the right process for taking decisions with such consequences.

Apart from the moral reason behind not jeopardizing the future rights of minorities, there is often a practical reason for not putting such emotive issues to vote. Which is that when a minority loses by a vote on such an issue it will not cooperate in its implementation. It may even feel compelled to resort to non-democratic, even violent, means to preserve its rights. (This was one of the factors leading to sectarian violence in Iraq following the first vote on the new constitution in which the Sunnis felt that the Shias, who were in the majority, had passed a constitution that was unfair to the Sunnis and could deprive the Sunnis of their share of national oil revenues, leading in due course to their economic and social decline.)

It is important for both moral as well as practical reasons that majorities do not unfairly hurt minorities even though majority rule may justify their action. For such practical reasons, even executive boards within corporations are sometimes reluctant to settle issues by vote, though this may seem an efficient way to conclude a debate. For example, it may be unwise to overrule the view of the sales division by a vote on a decision in which the sales division is required to make substantial changes to its operations for the decision to succeed. Therefore, even within corporations, as in democracies, there are many situations in which consensus must be obtained rather than simply applying the rule of the majority.

The problem with consensus that both executives and politicians experience is that it seems impossible to get everyone to agree. Therefore, it is important to understand when consensus is required and, if so, how to obtain it. Though the expression 'win/win' is generally used when describing consensus, consensus (as distinguished from unanimity) aims for a 'win/not lose' outcome whereby those who do not win also do not lose something that matters greatly to them. The outcome of consensus must be distinguished from the outcome of a majority vote on one hand

and unanimity on the other. Majority votes result in 'win/lose' outcomes, while unanimity is the pursuit of 'win/win' outcomes that are not always possible or perhaps necessary.

Consensus requires that the aspirations and fears of all involved must be known so that the implications of the compromises that may have to be made are understood. A solution that threatens the minority, which is a 'win-lose' solution, cannot be accepted if consensus is desired. The effort must be to find a solution—stimulated by imitation, adaptation or creation of ideas—whereby the decision is supported by many who will have the passion to make it succeed and, at the same time, it will not be obstructed by others who, though they may not have the same passion for it, will not fear its outcome. This is the 'win/not lose' outcome that consensus must aim for.

Unanimity

Unanimity, a condition in which everyone involved has a lot of passion for a particular solution, seems rarely possible. Fortunately, there are very few situations in which it is essential to have unanimity. Consensus, as defined above, is often sufficient. When unanimity is necessary, deep fears if any should be known, and risks that each will be taking must be understood and willingly accepted. To obtain unanimity, it is often necessary to bring to the surface deeply held beliefs and build stronger bridges between people.

The few situations in which unanimity may be advisable is when those involved may be required to risk their lives and the absence of passionate commitment by any one member of the group may be dangerous for others. An example is a small mountaineering team choosing a risky and uncharted path to the summit. Everyone must have a great passion for the goal. All must be willing to risk their own lives if necessary to support another in danger. They must trust each other completely. There are very few such situations. Therefore, unanimity is not often necessary; consensus is sufficient.

'Plop'

'Plop' is the default process by which decisions are taken when the correct process is not applied for the desired outcome. If thought is not given beforehand to what is the appropriate decision process to obtain the desired outcome, effective decisions are not, and cannot, be reached. For each decision, the appropriate process from the four described earlier must be selected and systematically applied. If this is not done, the outcome will be insufficient support for the decision, as it was for the chairmen of the residents' association mentioned before. The decisions they announced at the meetings ended in plops. They were not supported in implementation and therefore the need to consider the decision came up again.

Skills to understand situations and to select the appropriate decision-making processes must be widespread in democracies. Because democracies require that many people should be involved with decisions that affect their lives, healthy democracies push participation in decision making down from the lofty portals of parliaments and legislative assemblies into many intermediate and local-level institutions. People in village panchayats, in urban residents' associations, and those working within public-private-people partnerships must learn to work democratically and effectively. Therefore, healthy democracies require that many people, not merely elected politicians, must have consensus building skills. If they do not, democracy can be a messy and often frustrating process.

THE TRIANGLE OF TRUST AND INTEGRITY

Growing mistrust in institutions, which was at the heart of the India scenarios, is leading more people to protest and prevent changes in policies proposed by government and advocated by business. Therefore, there is a policy logjam, the root cause of which is public mistrust of institutions. The condition of the country's institutions must be improved to pick up again the pace of India's economic growth and to sustain it.

Institutional reform is necessary not only in government and political parties, but business too. Unfortunately, the evidence around the world is that the pace at which business institutions are reforming themselves to meet the 21st century requirements of society is not sufficient. The World Values Survey provides a reliable source of changing national values. Between 1989 and 2007, it has periodically sampled the views of Indians towards business. In recent years, the attitudes of Indians as a whole have moved in an anti-business direction. On the question of whether private or government ownership of industry is to be preferred, support for private ownership doubled between 1989 and 2007 (from 11.2 to 23.2 per cent). But it tripled for government ownership (from 11.4 to 33.1 per cent). This would surprise people in the business world, who mix with people like themselves and pay attention only to those television channels and parts of the media they like.

The conclusion is that leaders of both business and government institutions must work much harder to win the trust of citizens. Trust in institutions requires leaders with integrity. Integrity has two dimensions. On one hand, integrity is the quality of being honest and uncompromising of values and principles. On this count many leaders of businesses, who were once admired for leading high performance companies and for creating shareholder value, such as Kenneth Lay of Enron and Rajat Gupta of McKinsey, have failed.

Integrity also means the quality of being integrated, of being in tune with and connected with the wider society. Leaders with great personal qualities of honesty can be deeply pained, and their businesses hurt, as the leaders of Shell were in Nigeria, when society questioned whether their business practices were in tune with society's evolving values. Very sadly, on this count, Prime Minister Manmohan Singh of India, widely admired for his personal integrity, proved to be a great disappointment to the people. He was seen by citizens as too remote, and seemingly too careless of their concerns about the deterioration of the fabric of the nation's institutions. Therefore, citizens lost trust in him to lead them any longer.

Three sets of institutions, often contending with each other, must collaborate to improve the world. They are governments, businesses and civil society. We saw the fault lines in their relationships in the image of the earthquake in Chapter 1. Governments are caught in the middle between the demands of business corporations for more freedom and the demands of civil society organizations for better governance and more regulation. The relationship between these three sets of institutions: governments, businesses and the people (whose aspirations and concerns are represented by myriad civil society organizations) can be depicted by a triangle, which I call the Triangle of Trust and Integrity (Figure 8.1).

Governments are always supposed to be for the people. This is rooted in their raison d'être—the reason for their existence. Now businesses are striving to explain why they are good for society. They are even beginning to espouse the mantra that they are the trustees of society's wealth. Businesses want to be free from the licenses and controls of government. They are realising that, ultimately, they need the license to operate from society.

Government and business should work together to develop policies and projects. There must be trust between them. The concept of 'Public-Private Partnerships' has caught on in many countries as a way to combine the resources and capabilities of governments and businesses to create and operate infrastructure

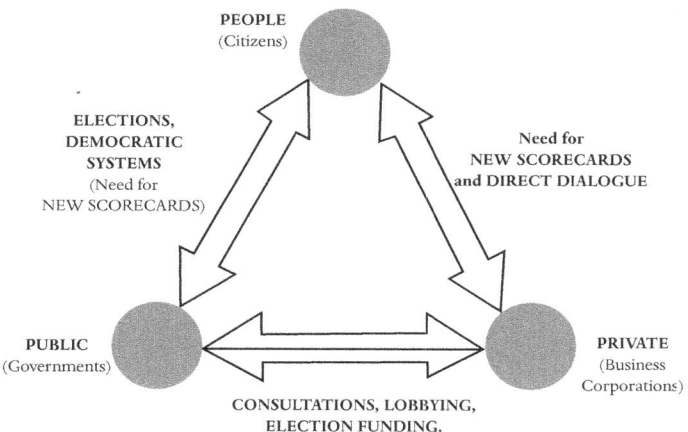

Figure 8.1: The Triangle of Trust and Integrity: Need for New Social Contracts

for the benefit of the people. However, the increasing closeness of government and corporations in the formulation of economic policies and in conceiving projects, with insufficient inclusion of people, results in perceptions of 'crony capitalism'.

When corporations are prevented from carrying on with their projects by resistance from local communities and civil society organizations, they turn to governments to clear the way for them. 'Explain to the people that we are good for them—that we create jobs, and we produce what people need,' say the corporations. In this way, corporations themselves reinsert governments into the equation though they would like governments to get out of their way. If citizens trusted corporations more, there would be less need for governments to intercede. For this, corporations must learn to win the trust of people. They must be more 'integrated' with society. They must listen to what people need and want; they must build these requirements into the conduct of their operations and design of their products; they must honestly and transparently report their performance on these measures to societal stakeholders.

Business managers operating in free and competitive markets must be very good at listening to and responding to their customers. Otherwise, their business would not survive. Economist Albert O. Hirschman observes, in his book *Exit, Voice, and Loyalty* (1970), that the more attention business managers pay to listening to customers and the better they get at it, the less capable they may become to hear the voices of citizens of society.

Hirschman points out that the way customers signal their displeasure to corporations is by not buying the firm's products—in other words, by 'exiting'. Their voice is clearly expressed—yea or nay—by their decision to purchase or not. On the other hand, citizens do not exit the system. Indeed they cannot because they cannot leave and they cannot be banished. If they are displeased, they may speak up. However, when they speak, what they are saying is not always clear. Nevertheless, as noted earlier, their displeasure can affect corporations' business performance in various ways and, therefore, business managers must try to understand civil society's concerns and expectations. Hirschman explains:

> Exit is the sort of mechanism economics thrives on. It is neat—one either exits or one does not; it is impersonal—any face-to-face confrontation between customer and firm is avoided. In all these respects, voice is just the opposite of exit. It is a far more 'messy' concept because it cannot be graduated, all the way from faint grumbling to violent protest; it implies articulation of one's critical opinions rather than a private, 'secret' vote in the anonymity of a supermarket. (ibid.: 15)

Hirschman points out that Milton Friedman, who famously decreed that the business of business must only be business, had expressed his difficulty in accepting the notion that people should desire to express their views to make them prevail. Friedman describes people's desire to be heard as a resort to 'cumbrous political channels'. He would much rather they resort to 'efficient market mechanisms' and use their money rather than their mouths to make their opinions known.

In the market, we are customers. In society, we are citizens. Good corporations know how to listen to their customers. Great corporations know also how to listen to citizens. For great corporations, the business of business cannot be only business: they also strive to perform their role as trustees of society. To perform their role as trustees, they need civil society to be their conscience, their canary in the mine, and their collaborator.

When governments and business leaders wish to work more closely with each other to shape economic policies, as they must, and to conceive Public-Private Partnership projects, it becomes imperative that the other two sides of the triangle of trust, between people and government, and between people and businesses, must become much stronger. Otherwise the suspicion of crony capitalism will arise.

The three points of the triangle of trust must connect for it to have integrity. Both the Public (government) and Private (business corporations) must connect with the People. Policies and projects must become People-Public-Private Partnerships (PPPP). For trust in institutions to be rebuilt, people must become a key partner in the social and economic contract.

The development of new scorecards that reflect what citizens really care about has become very urgent for both business corporations and governments. Governments and businesses must reach out to people and establish processes for a continuing dialogue. Scorecards must embody the contract between the people and the institutions they give their trust to.

9

HOW ON EARTH CAN WE LIVE TOGETHER

How can a part know the whole? Man is related to everything that he knows. And everything is both cause and effect, working and worked upon, mediate and intermediate, all things mutually dependent.

—BLAISE PASCAL

The design of a house provides spaces for its occupants' needs. Processes of interactions amongst its occupants determine how well the house turns into a home. The wiring in the house enables its occupants to connect their utilities, and technology can also enable communication amongst them. In the same ways, as we saw in previous chapters, democracies require structures, and processes of communication and decision making. Technology can facilitate these processes.

In this chapter, we examine how technology can assist processes of communication and decision making. A macro-level architecture of institutions is described to enable the performance of functions that have become necessary for 21st century governance requirements. This institutional architecture will also conform to the principles of complex self-adaptive systems described in Chapter 4.

TECHNOLOGY AND WIRING OF THE HOUSE

'E-governance' has become a buzzword. Technology firms are winning huge e-governance contracts from governments in many countries. E-governance may be a misnomer for what firms and governments are actually doing. With e-governance, governments are improving service delivery to citizens. Governments are also improving their internal efficiencies. Thus e-governance is like the wiring of the house that enables citizens to connect their appliances easily and transports electricity around the house efficiently. 'Governance', on the other hand, is a process of making change, shaping policies and taking decisions. What is called 'e-governance' may be better described as 'e-government', since it deals almost entirely with delivery of services by the government, rather than processes of governance. In designing e-government processes, it seems best to eliminate human interference, whereas for good democratic governance, citizens should speak and be heard.

Technology, especially communication technologies, such as the Internet, social media and mobile phones, can play roles in governance. They can improve communications amongst citizens, and they can facilitate processes of democratic deliberation and decision making. Let us examine the possibilities that technology provides for governance.

Shortly after the tragedy of 9/11, Donald Rumsfeld, United States (US) Secretary of Defense, was asked by reporters why the US, with its mighty defence arsenal equipped with the latest technologies, could not prevent the horrific attacks. He replied that when anyone, from anywhere, using any means available can strike you, how can you prevent it. He was pointing to the ease with which people can travel, communicate and send money anywhere, using public transport, public communications and the Internet, as the terrorists had done. This is the flip side of the benefits of technology.

On 26 November 2008, ten terrorists from Pakistan struck at several places in Mumbai, killing over 170 people, and wounding another 300. One of these sites was the luxury Taj Mahal Hotel. Here, four gunmen entered the hotel and roamed within it for fifty-eight hours. Thirty-three persons died in the hotel, scores were injured, and the hotel was set ablaze. Their handlers, back in Pakistan, had mobile phones, computers, television monitors and detailed maps of the city and even of the Taj Mahal Hotel.

Cathy Scott-Clark and Adrian Levy recount what happened in the hotel in their gripping book, *The Siege: 68 Hours Inside the Taj* (2013). They describe how technology and terror mingled during this horror show. Google Earth and a Garmin GPS were used to plan the strikes on Mumbai. Inside the Taj, the frightened guests called, texted and tweeted throughout the attack, often providing their assailants with deadly real-time information. In one remarkable scene, a hostage is taken (Ram), and the attackers report his name back to their controllers, who Google him and do an image search.

Here is the author's account of the conversation that transpired:

> 'O.K., listen, is he wearing glasses?' He was. 'He is balding at the front?' Umer (a gunman) shouted at Ram: 'Hold your head straight.' Umer replied: 'Yes, yes, he is bald. He's got a face like a dog.' Qahafa (a handler in Pakistan) had found Ram's online résumé. A top-class hostage. He was pleased.

The authors of *The Siege* fear 'the next wave of terrorists, who will come wearing Google glass'.

All technology is 'dual use'. It can be used for benign as well as evil purposes. How can one prevent its misuse? Governments try, and indeed they must, to ensure the safety of their citizens. But, in attempting to do this, they curb liberties and invade privacies. When the Chinese government curbs its citizens' access to the Internet and restricts the operations of US Internet service providers in China, the US government protests. Then the US government itself is exposed for using its massive technology apparatus to invade the privacies of citizens all over the world, even heads of state of foreign countries!

Can new Internet and mobile phone based communications technologies, with their immense reach, enable these agreements to be reached? Not by themselves. They can be used to stir up hate as easily, or more easily perhaps, as they can be used to raise people's aspirations for a common good.

Technology will not, by itself, create a better world. It is only an instrument to be used, to create the world we want to live in. What are the values we wish to live by? And, what means are acceptable to produce the outcomes we want? These moral questions will always remain to be answered even when we develop amazing technologies. In fact, as technology develops further, the need for agreements about these moral issues amongst governments and people all around the world is becoming ever more urgent.

In the 1990s, computation and communication technologies began to be layered into organizations. Many consultants sold them as the panacea for business organizations' competitiveness. Organizations spent millions of dollars on technology. Much of it was wasted till it was realized that *business processes* must be redesigned to improve business performance and that technology can only be an enabler.

So it is with communications too. The *process* of communication must be first designed to fulfil the purpose for which it is intended. Then technology can be used to speed up the steps in the process.

PROCESSES FOR DEMOCRATIC DELIBERATION

Democracies of elites or opinion leaders, who debate and decide amongst themselves what is best for the people, are at best a democracy *for* the people. A democracy *by* the people requires their participation in the deliberations. It is practically very difficult to include everyone, or even many people in deliberations. Technology seems to provide possibilities for including masses of people in democratic deliberation. Experience shows that the vast reach of technology can also make democratic deliberation more difficult.

The Internet, social media and mobile phones bombard us with thousands of bits of information, messages and tweets. It is difficult for anyone to keep in touch with everyone and everything. If we are connected, we suffer from an 'attention deficit disorder'. Coping strategies are: remain on all the time; pay shallow attention to many things; and choose the many we wish to follow from the millions we can. All these strategies make a deeper understanding of others impossible.

Remaining on all the time with shallow attention reduces the depth at which we are with others. People meet to have coffee together. Everyone is looking into their smart phones, and not at each other. People together at a business meeting keep one eye on their smart phone or iPad on the table, and the other to dip in an out of what is happening in the room. Internet and social media have vast 'reach', but staying connected reduces the 'richness' of conversations amongst people.

The third coping strategy, of choosing websites, tweeters and Facebook friends one will follow, as perforce one must, makes us stay with people we like because they are like us. We easily understand what they say. If we have to make an extra effort to understand something or someone, we just shut them out. There is no time to reflect. Thus we get locked within 'conceptually gated communities'. Across the walls are others in their own resonance chambers like we are, hearing what they like, and listening to who they like.

The divides of ideology and beliefs that separate people can be bridged only when people listen to each other deeply: to 'why' the other believes what she believes; to 'who' she is; and not merely to 'what' she says. People must look each other in the eyes to see the persons behind the words.

The methods we have to communicate with each other can be described along a continuum of diminishing 'richness' with increasing 'reach'. On one end is a dialogue between two persons— very rich, but with reach only to one other. At the other end we have the online reach of the Internet and social media—vast reach, but very shallow communication. In between are 'vision workshops' of dozens of people, and 'large group interactive processes' of perhaps hundreds, and many other such formats. These are designed for deeper deliberations than in conventional business and citizen meetings, and to enable agreements about visions and principles that can only be scratched at in the formality of conventional meetings.

A selection of formats of meetings for bringing people together, from across the continuum of richness and reach, can be combined into larger processes for democratic deliberation. These processes must adhere to some basic principles of inclusive, deliberative democracy. James Fishkin, professor of communication and political science at Stanford University, describes three principles in his book, *When the People Speak: Deliberative Democracy and Public Consultation* (2009). He says a good process must fulfil three norms: political equality, deliberation and mass participation.

The first norm, political equality, requires that all who participate are considered equal in the deliberations. Those who have more—power, wealth or education—must not overpower the voices of others. This is not easy because we are habituated to defer to them.

The second norm, deliberation, requires that people have the information required, that they listen to other points of view, and that they are able to advocate their own views too without being intimidated by the power of others. The conversations must be 'rich' in content, and in understanding of issues and of others.

The third norm, mass participation, requires reach for many to be engaged—perhaps too many to enable richness in the deliberations.

Humanity's aspirations are reaching much higher than they were at the time of Athenian democracy. The processes of democratic discussion that Athenians used, which for a long time have inspired Western democracies, are now considered faulty. They emphasized deliberation, but did not meet the requirement of political equality and mass participation. For instance, women and slaves were excluded from participation.

The founders of the US Constitution were acutely aware of the need for suitable processes for democratic deliberation. Such processes would be necessary to implement their vision of 'government of the people, for the people, and *by* the people' too. James Madison (fourth president of the US, hailed as the 'Father of the Constitution' and the key champion and author of the United States Bill of Rights), described what was required, and what the difficulties were in devising a good process, in *The Federalist Papers*. Madison wrote in *The Federalist* No. 55: 'had every Athenian citizen been a Socrates, every Athenian assembly would still have been a mob'. Thereby he pointed to the need for a good process. In *The Federalist* No. 10 he wrote about the need for taking 'raw' opinions from the people and 'refining' them in bodies of elected representatives.

Madison and the other framers of the US Constitution would

be distressed to read Jeffrey Sachs' comment on the state of affairs in the US at the start of the 21st century. In his book, *The Price of Civilization: Economics and Ethics after the Fall* (2011), Sachs, director of the Earth Institute at Columbia University, laments that in America today, there is little systematic public deliberation and the public's views are not taken seriously in the political process. He says that policy decisions are being adopted behind the backs of the public, often in direct contradiction to public opinion.

How should raw public opinions be gathered, and what should be the design of processes for their refinement? These are critical issues in designing processes for democratic deliberation in the 21st century. The mass of shallow information that comes from social media is too raw and not sufficiently ripe for refinement by Elite Deliberation (as Madison called it) in national assemblies of elected representatives in large countries.

It is difficult to design an ideal process that fulfils the three norms Fishkin admits. He recommends that institutions should be created to research, experiment and develop new processes. At the Center for Deliberative Democracy in Stanford, Fishkin has been experimenting with a process he describes as Deliberative Polling, which he has tried in many countries, including the US, UK, Japan, and China. Another such institution is the Danish Board of Technology, an office set up by the Danish Parliament to offer continuing capacity to sponsor deliberative consultations. In its case, it is pursuing the concept of 'consensus conferences' which has been applied in many settings.

India, a vast, diverse democracy, has great need for good processes for democratic deliberation to create a vision to guide its progress and to shape its plans. Many processes are being tried and research into processes is underway. The Centre for Internet and Society in Bangalore is researching ways in which the Internet and social media can facilitate democratic deliberations. The Planning

Commission constructed a process which combined techniques at both ends of the 'richness-reach' continuum to get inputs for the preparation of India's 12th Five Year Plan. Around 950 civil society organizations, representing a diversity of constituents—women, youth, scheduled castes and tribes, the minority religions, urban poor, children, and transgenders—fanned out to garner the opinions of their members. The Internet and social media was used to obtain inputs of those who have access to these mediums.

Another large initiative was taken up by *Rajasthan Patrika*, a Hindi language newspaper with twenty-three million readers in eight Indian states. *Patrika* designed a process for three Indian states that were going into elections in late 2013: Rajasthan, Madhya Pradesh and Chhattisgarh. In each of these states, citizens in every constituency participated to create a vision for their constituency and their state. Ten stakeholder groups were identified. Separate meetings were held with each of these ten groups in each of the 520 constituencies in these three states, a total of 5,200 meetings. In each meeting, in a structured process, citizens discussed their concerns, their requirements and their vision. The output of these meetings have been compiled and given to all political parties contesting the elections. Thus, politicians have heard the voices of the people they will represent if they win the elections.

THE DESIGN OF THE HOUSE

Good deliberations amongst citizens are necessary for a good democratic home. Also, the house must be designed to provide them with the spaces they need to do their work. I describe here six macro-level architectural principles to shape institutional spaces and processes for governance in an interconnected and complex world. The six principles are labelled the 'Six Ls' for ease of recollection.

Listening

The first 'L' is Listening. The world has become exponentially more interconnected in the last two decades than it has ever been. Human aspirations have increased, and so has the human population. The pressure humanity is putting on the earth has become unbearable. Impatience with the pace of 'trickle-down' and increasing value for human rights is straining prevalent approaches to economic growth and development. To live together we must listen to each other. However, the means of communication that are connecting us with their enormous 'reach', while making it more necessary for us to understand each other are also making it more difficult. Therefore, we must counter their shallowness with processes that add richness to our deliberations. Richness in our deliberations comes from listening to each other more deeply. Processes to enable more richness along with reach must be an essential component of the design of a better home, as we have already discussed.

Localization

Localization is a key design requirement for 'complex self-adaptive systems'.

Consider the Amazon forest. It is perhaps the richest ecosystem on earth—dense with a large variety of vegetation, swarming with many species of reptiles and animals, humming with many species of birds and insects. It works. It renews itself. Who is in charge? No one body. Each part of the system—each tree and plant, each animal and reptile, each bird and insect—supports each other in complex ways not completely understood. And each of these billions of entities is a self-complete functioning organization.

Complex self-adaptive ecosystems are richer when they have more diversity and when diversity combines at smaller scales.

Scientific forestry and scientific agriculture increase yields of single species with the planting of a single species on large tracts of land. But these scientific approaches reduce the ability of an ecosystem to renew itself. Therefore, more inputs have to be put in from outside—fertilizer, pesticides, even seeds.

The founders of the US Constitution understood the need for local self-governing communities. They believed that such organizations would produce better outcomes for communities. They also appreciated the opportunities that such locally managed communities provide for developing civic-minded citizens who are the fundamental constituents of a democratic republic. Mahatma Gandhi promoted the idea of self-governing villages for the same reasons.

There are practical reasons why localization produces better results. Solutions that are produced locally fit local contexts. There are also normative reasons for advocating localization. People should be in charge of their own affairs. Yet many policymakers and academicians do not support this idea. They fear the chaos that could result if local communities begin to do their 'own thing'. They also point to the many failed experiences of local governance.

The fear of what these control-minded people describe as chaos arises from their mental model of what a well governed system should be like. In their model, a city should be planned from above, with its parts separated for different functions. In their view, a scientific forest is better organized than the complex, dense Amazon forest.

No doubt, many schemes of local governance have failed. But, at the same time, there are many examples of successful, locally managed cities and villages in many countries. Sceptics should look at *how* they work and *why* they work. Perhaps the desire of those in charge at the top to stay 'in control', and their unwillingness to promote and support localization, could be reasons why the many attempts to introduce localization have failed. The 'controllers' do not pass down the resources required, nor give adequate freedom from their centrally devised rules.

These are some of the reasons why localization is not succeeding in India, even though it is very necessary in a country as large and as diverse as it is. It is also a country committed to the normative benefits of localization, viz. empowering people and giving them more freedom to manage their own affairs. In fact, localization is the key to two of the three strategies for faster, more inclusive and sustainable development that were distilled from the India scenarios described in Chapter 2.

Full empowerment comes not from delegation alone. It also requires citizens to have the ability to manage their affairs. They must learn to listen to each other. They should be able to map and understand the whole system they are responsible for. India has determined to make local-level 'spatial' planning of cities, with citizens' participation a mandatory condition for towns and cities to qualify for government financial assistance in future. Such spatial plans must consider all essential services and also the patterns of economic and social activities. National programmes will provide (through the states) guidance to citizens and local government functionaries about how to make their plans. Local functionaries must have the technical and managerial skills required too. The Indian government is rolling out a country-wide process to provide them with 'just-in-time' and 'task-aligned' training.

For localization to work, not only will local-level functionaries and citizens have to learn new skills. Central managers will have to learn new theories and shed the old ones about how to manage large systems and 'scale up' results. They will have to learn to 'spread around' learning and power, rather than concentrating it at the centre.

Lateralization

Localization's indispensable companion structures in complex self-adaptive systems are lateral links between local organizations. The principle of 'permeable' boundaries' requires that local organizations, while maintaining their own integrity, be open to inputs from other organizations. The Second Law of Thermodynamics explains that 'in closed systems' the entropy (useless energy) of the system will inevitably increase with time. Therefore, interactions with other organizations are required as this enables exchanges and combinations of resources and provides opportunities to learn from others too.

Laterally oriented organizations value collaboration and learning, whereas vertically oriented hierarchical organizations are designed for better control. In the latter, large bureaucracies are divided into vertical silos, each specializing in one function, and each looking upwards for direction rather than cooperating laterally with other specializations to address systemic issues where collaboration amongst many is necessary.

'Communities of practice' in development and consulting organizations cut across internal organizational boundaries. Similarly, communities of practice can be created amongst villages in a state, and even the whole country. Many small enterprises that operate in clusters can share resources, and learn from each other, and thus become very competitive, even against much larger monolithic organizations. Organization design, like communications tools, is also a 'dual use' technology. Terrorism networks use principles of localization combined with lateral links to powerful effect against large establishments of security forces. They prove the power of lateralization combined with localization. We also must use it more purposefully to create the good world we want.

The benefits of globalization and also the benefits of internet-based communications lie in the increased possibilities of lateralization of many systems and processes. These developments can be taken advantage of to construct efficient learning platforms, for example, between cities in the same country and in other countries too. Such lateral links are developing at the city level, beneath the levels of state and national governments. Learning about better practices of city government and sustainable technologies is spreading across these networks. For example, the Euro-India Center, a non-governmental organization (NGO), is bringing officials and businesses from European and Indian cities together. The United Nations Development Plan's (UNDP's) Solution Exchange is an Internet-enabled platform that brings practitioners and academics together to share ideas on development issues. Such learning platforms are puncturing national and state boundaries thus making them more permeable.

Dee Hock, founder of the Visa networked payment system, which was an early exemplar of the power of the principles of localization combined with lateralization, writes in his book, *One From Many: VISA and the Rise of Chaordic Organization* (2005: 225):

> Changes in existing organizations and the evolution of wholly new ones will have many characteristics in common. Just as the human body is not a vertical hierarchy with each part superior to another in ascending, linear order, organizations of the future will not be structured. Great pyramids of superiors and subordinates will yield to affiliations of semi-independent equals, whether they be individuals within an organization, or organizations within a larger whole.

Learning

The fourth 'L' is Learning which, with Listening, is the other soft structure, equally essential for a complex self-adaptive system.

Nations progress by learning to do what they could not do before. In the 19th century, industrialization enabled Western nations to grow their economies much faster than others. In the 20th century, industrialization propelled Japan's, Taiwan's and Korea's growth. In the 21st century, China has lifted millions out of poverty by rapid industrialization. Industrialization is a process of nations learning to do more complex things. At the same time, human development indicators improve when nations learn to provide health and education more effectively than before. Economies grow, incomes grow, and human development indicators improve when nations learn more. They succeed in international competition when they learn and implement faster than others.

If we can manage only what we can measure, how shall we measure the learning of organizations and other large institutions? Ray Stata, founder of Analog Devices, a Massachusetts-based company, which is a world leader in the production of high-tech communication and electronic equipment, has introduced a simple measure. Since learning is the ability to produce more complex products or perform more complex tasks, Stata developed the concept of the 'half-life of learning'. The half-life is a concept used in the measurement of radiation. The intensity of radiation reduces exponentially as the source depletes. Therefore, a measure of the time it takes to reduce radiation levels by half is a good measure of the strength of the source.

Institutions can set themselves time targets to 'learn' new capabilities. They should determine what the gap is between their present capability and what they intend to do. This will enable them to measure their progress towards the target. Generally, improvement becomes more difficult as one approaches later and more difficult stages. Therefore, Stata proposed that it was sufficient to know how long it takes to reach the half-way capability of a development mark, whatever the end goal, to gauge the speed at which the organization is able to learn.

We have discussed balanced scorecards earlier with four domains: economic measures, sustainability measures, measures of 'inclusion', and measures of governance. Goals must be set in all these domains. Another instrument can also be designed for the dashboard, which will show the pace at which the institution—nation or business organization—is achieving progress against its goals. This would indicate the pace at which the institution is learning. If other organizations are learning faster, one could study them to learn about learning.

All the other five 'Ls' in the framework can enable better and faster learning. So far, we have seen how Listening, Localization and Lateralization enable learning in the system. We will soon see how the remaining two Ls can be oriented for learning too.

Leadership

Leadership is considered indispensable for making change happen. There are many forms and models of leadership. Thousands of books have been written on the subject, and I will not dwell too long on it. However, I will point out the essential function that leadership performs in a complex self-adaptive system.

Recollect the description of the complex self-adapting Amazon forest. The question asked was, 'Who is in charge?' The answer was, seemingly nobody. Most human institutions are not run in this way. Someone is the boss. She or he needs to be in control. Power is centralized. The organization is not localized. The organization works in silos. It is not as lateralized. The qualities of listening and learning are neither measured nor even observed. If the aeroplane must be redesigned while it is flying, a leader's responsibility is to put processes for Listening, Localization, Lateralization, and Learning into the institution.

To accomplish this, the leader must have a vision of the end state that is desired. This vision should also be understood by the other crew and the passengers in the aircraft. They should see how the redesign will benefit them. They should understand the risks, too, and the roles they will play in managing those risks.

The change will require people to give up old ways of thinking and acting and adopt new ways of thinking and acting. It is generally believed that unless people change their ways of thinking, they will not change their ways of working. However, more often people act themselves into new ways of thinking, than think themselves into new ways of acting. There is a reason for this. Our ways of working are based on 'theories-in-use' in the backs of our minds. Our ways of acting have worked for us so far. Therefore, we believe the theory. If different actions were to produce even better results for us, we may be willing to unlearn the old theory and make room for a new one in our minds.

Successful leaders of change programmes understand this. They nudge people in the organization to act like they should in the new vision. They encourage them to try the new ways, and they enable them to learn new skills. Change leaders notice early successes and propagate them through the organization so that more people can learn and the change is reinforced.

Charles Sabel, professor of law and social science at Columbia University, has focused his research on innovations in governance. He has examined processes in several countries by which change has been brought about from centrally controlled methods to more locally empowered and laterally connected processes. He says that successful change of complex systems is driven by a 'learning forward' philosophy. There is a vision towards which the system is moving. It keeps acting and entering new territories of knowledge and capability. It then makes the new ways of working that succeed its new culture—its new way of doing things.

Prof Sabel has observed that leaders in such successful processes exercise a 'contingent power'. They do not tell the 'locals', who must acquire new capabilities, what to do. They resist giving the solution. They challenge the locals to do better. Most importantly, they enable the locals to learn by shaping the institutional structures and processes required for this.

It has become customary to refer to anyone with a high position as a leader. We refer to anyone who has been raised onto a pedestal as a leader. Thus all chief executive officers (CEOs) are called business leaders. And all heads of government institutions are also called leaders. Great leaders improve the condition of the institutions they lead while they are also on the pedestal. Whereas others, who are leaders in name only, enjoy the visibility they get on their pedestals. They leave the institutions atop which they sit in no better condition when they depart.

Locus

I have chosen an unusual name for the sixth structure required for complex self-adaptive institutions. I did not want to use any of the usual terms, such as office, unit or commission, because this structure is an unusual one. The term 'Locus' does well enough. It suggests that somewhere in the system something is being done. What is this?

Jeffrey Sachs writes in *The Price of Civilization* (2011: 177):

> The sad truth about Washington today is that we lack serious institutions charged with carrying out systematic planning for the future. The Office of Management and

> Budget prepares federal budget proposals one year at a time. The US Treasury has little capacity or mandate to undertake long-term economic strategy. There is no coordinating agency for public investments by the federal government, nor is there a planning agency, as in many other countries... The Governments' departments are organized along the traditional lines that reflect the era when issues hit the American political scene, not the cross-cutting challenges we face today....All these problems of short-termism are compounded by an anti-planning mentality... The *key* to effective planning is to embrace complexity. ...Plans are vital, but they must include several inter-linked policies, be adaptive over time, and be open to a wide range of participants from business, government agencies, and civil society organizations... Upgrading OMB or another agency to prepare multi-year plans will sound heretical to most Americans.

I quote extensively from Sachs' book to make the point that the US, a bastion of pro-marketism, anti-governmentism and anti-planning, is feeling the need for some 'process' and some 'organization' to guide a participative process to make sense of the future and guide collective action. US policymakers and economists who advise them have dismissed 'industrial policy' as a Soviet-era invention to be consigned to history's dustbin. Prof Ha-Joon Chang, Reader in Political Economy of Development at University of Cambridge, says that US industrial policy has been to tell every other nation that they must not have an industrial policy. Now the US is feeling the need for a government-led formulation of industrial policy to create more jobs in the country.

On the other hand, India, which has a Planning Commission looking ahead and making five year plans for the country since

1951, and had 'industrial policies' until the 1990s, has become disenchanted with planning and with industrial policy. It needs growth of industries and creation of jobs (for its burgeoning population of youth), much more than the US! India also feels the need for better management of its development process. What India has realized is that its problems with planning and industrial policy are the approach it had taken to these activities.

National planning and industrial policymaking cannot be top-down activities undertaken in government offices in New Delhi or Washington. They must be dynamic and participative processes. India's Planning Commission has taken a fresh outside-in look at its planning process (as mentioned in Chapter 2). The Planning Commission has also examined the need to reformulate the purpose and the process of industrial policymaking. It studied the experiences of many other countries that have successfully grown their industries through processes of rapid capability building. These include Japan, Korea and China. It also examined countries that continue to maintain competitive advantages in manufacturing industries, especially Germany and Japan, in spite of high wages and very strong currencies (both of which are considered to be big handicaps for manufacturing competitiveness). These studies have revealed that planning and industrial policymaking processes are successful when they are oriented towards stimulating faster learning in the country

When change is fast and unpredictable, when election cycles are short as they are in the US (two years) and India (two to three years at most with state elections between five-year national election cycles), when politics is competitive, then the need becomes palpable for some national 'process' that 'guides' a flotilla of independent boats—many agencies in the central government; agencies in many state governments; and many independent organizations in the private sector.

How do you guide the captains of independent boats (or pilots of independent aeroplanes) to follow the same general course? A widely respected Indian industrialist (and a keen pilot himself) suggested a new role for the Planning Commission. He suggested it should provide a radar map of the conditions ahead. The pilots of aeroplanes (and captains of boats) can use this to steer their crafts safely. The scenario planning process the Indian Planning Commission has adopted for the first time to supplement the preparation of the 12th Five Year Plan provides such a radar map. It guides policymakers to the best channels to take—the strategies to adopt to realize faster, more inclusive and sustainable growth in uncertain global conditions.

When the prime minister of India received the outcome of the outside-in review of India's Planning Commission in 2010, he summarized that the Planning Commission must become a *systems' reform commission*, and not an allocator of funds and reviewer of plans and projects made by central government ministries and Indian state governments.

This begs the following question: what is the purpose of the systems that are required? Should they be designed to enable more control over the system, or should they enable faster learning? Is the role of the central organization that is responsible for systems' reforms to be akin to a 'head' office or to a 'help' office? The knowledge and skills required to enable learning in the system are different to those required for controlling the system. Even the orientations of the officers in this organization towards others in the system would be different depending on the role it is expected to play.

The best location of this organization would appear to be at the top, beside the chief executive. However, it must see beyond the term of the executive and have the courage to recommend the best long-term course for the country. Its loyalty must be to the system and not the executive. Therefore, a system design question, in a parliamentary system, is: should it be a constitutional body accountable to parliament and not the executive? The location of this reforming unit which provides learning, stimulation, and systems reform must fit the political structure of the country. There cannot be a one-size fits all recommendation for its location or its design. Each country will have to find its own answers.

The World Bank organized a revealing seminar in Washington in October 2013 to examine the development and growth of nations through the lens of their capacity to learn. A paper by Luke Jordan of the World Bank, and Sébastien Turban and Laurence Wilse-Samson of Columbia University, presented a new framework for the study of 'state learning'. It examines three components of 'state learning': the generation of new information, the transmission of that knowledge upwards and horizontally across the system, and acting upon that information ('implementation'). Then it considers the comparative setting of China and India for an empirical comparison of the framework (Jordan et al., 2013).

China has achieved much more than India in the last twenty years in terms of both economic growth and human development indicators. Per capita incomes have increased four and a half times faster in China than India since 1979.

Some of the explanations given by the authors are:

1. In *public administration* China has undertaken reform once every five years since 1978, while India has only attempted it twice in sixty-five years, with the last attempt (the Second Administrative Reforms Commission) still unimplemented. Thus China has been continuously tuning up the capacity of the state to learn and deliver. In India, substantial institutional reforms are overdue.
2. China has *think tanks* with their units spread in its provinces

observing and explaining change. India's think tanks are concentrated in Delhi and they do more theoretical work.
3. China effectively uses its *federal structure as a means for learning* through experiments in its provinces and cities, comparisons amongst them, and distribution of the best practices learned. India's federal system operates as a hub-and-spoke system between the centre and the states. The centre has yet to develop effective platforms to support lateral inter-state learning.
4. China has a far more effective *'HR' management system for its bureaucracy* than India. For example, promotions in China are based on 360-degree appraisals. In India, confidential reports by superiors are the means of assessment. Chinese bureaucrats are judged on performance. Tenures of Indian bureaucrats are too short to make such judgements.

Both countries have been preparing national plans for over sixty years. India's plans are made by its Planning Commission, while China's plans are made by its National Development and Reform Commission. The names of the two organizations reveal their orientations—one for planning, the other for development and reform. The authors have not examined this angle, but it is worth exploring.

Malaysia has been preparing five year plans for almost as long as India and China. The country's plans are prepared by the Economic Planning Unit in the Prime Minister's Office. In 2009, Malaysia established PEMANDU, the Performance Management Delivery Unit in the Prime Minister's Office. This unit facilitates the creation of visions and action plans by stakeholders for various sectors of the economy. It supports the deputy prime minister and prime minister in monitoring progress. Prof Charles Sabel of Columbia, who has studied PEMANDU, suggests that the prime minister and deputy prime minister exercise their 'contingent powers' only in PEMANDU, to give impetus to the stakeholders to find solutions to improve performance. The results so far seem promising.

Many other countries have central bodies fulfilling some roles of planning, or evaluating, or knowledge gathering. The role of the Ministry of International Trade and Industry (MITI) in the rapid development of Japan has been well researched and reported. The Korean Development Institute, Bhutan's Gross National Happiness Commission, South Africa's National Planning Commission, Finland's Innovation Council, and the Philippines' National Competitiveness Council are some other examples of central organizations with responsibilities for guiding national development. The locations of such central organizations in the political and government systems of their country differ as do their roles.

All six structures in any country, the six Ls, must be aligned with each other for the system to have integrity. Therefore, there cannot be a standard blueprint for any of them, only general principles. The precise design of each must fit into the arrangement of the others at all times or else the aeroplane cannot keep flying. Therefore all must evolve together. This is the essential requirement for designing an aeroplane while it is flying.

10

VISIONS OF THE FUTURE

Where there is no vision, the people perish.

—PROVERB 24:18, THE OLD TESTAMENT

The problems we face cannot be solved by following the same approach that has caused our problems, Albert Einstein observed. Humanity is becoming concerned about the impact the paradigm of relentless material growth has had on the earth. The earth's atmosphere, rivers, forests, soil, and oceans cannot take the burden much longer. Impatience with the pace of 'trickle-down' growth economics is increasing fast. We need another way to shape our societies.

Whenever we feel the need for change we yearn for good leadership. The leaders who appear turn out to be more of the same. People rise up to overthrow dictators. Often chaos follows. Then they yearn for a strong, steadying hand. And another dictator rises. The pendulum swings from chaos to stasis and to chaos again. In between chaotic systems and centrally engineered systems lies the space of complex self-adaptive systems. The principles by which such systems operate have been described in this book. These principles have been applied to formulate the architectural principles with which 21st century institutions of governance should be shaped. A structure of institutions, 'the 6 Ls', is explained in the previous chapter.

How successful leaders operate must be congruent with the nature of the process they must lead. Conductors of symphony orchestras operate differently to leaders of jazz combos because the process of producing music in a symphony is very different to the process by which a jazz combo makes music.

Paradigms of leadership must be congruent with paradigms of change. A picture can say more than a thousand words. In this chapter, four paradigms about how change is brought about in large systems are presented through four evocative pictures. In each picture, the paradigm of leadership that goes with the paradigm of change is visible. These scenarios of change and leadership were developed in India in 2000, by a large, very diverse group of persons who were concerned about the future of their country. The models of change and leadership they describe are seminal and have universal application. The paradigms of change illustrated by these scenarios provided the foundations for the India scenarios prepared by the World Economic Forum in 2005. They also underlie the three scenarios prepared by the Planning Commission in 2012 which were presented in Chapter 2. In fact the pictures can be seen lurking behind the three scenarios in *Figure 2.5: The Keys to Produce the Scenario we want*.

SCENARIO I: BUFFALOES WALLOWING

Buffaloes cooling themselves in a pond is a familiar sight in the Indian countryside—it is difficult for any of them to move because they are surrounded by other buffaloes. In this scenario, experts, bureaucrats and others in prominent positions are expected to determine policies and bring about changes. We loosely describe such people as 'leaders' regardless of how effective (or ineffective) they are. They cannot agree on what should be done; what one

Figure 10.1: Buffaloes Wallowing (Scenario I)
The buffaloes continue to wallow in the swamp. It is time to move on. Who can goad them? The boy herding the buffaloes yells to them that they will go hungry if they do not make a move. One or two attempt to get out of the water, but they are surrounded by others. So they give up.

proposes, others oppose, and nothing much happens. Meanwhile, the children in India—its' 'demographic dividend' on which economists base future high gross domestic product (GDP) growth rates—are awaiting improvements in health care and education, and opportunities to work gainfully when they grow up. Improvements are being made but they are too slow.

Every worthwhile solution seems to require many people to act together, whether it is in education, rural development or industrial growth. Government, businesses and communities, all have a role to play. In living rooms and conference halls, people describe the grand solutions. And they also are frustrated by their inability to implement them.

SCENARIO II: PEACOCKS STRUTTING

Figure 10.2: Peacocks Strutting and Birds Scrambling (Scenario II)
Grain is strewn in the courtyard for the birds. They have been waiting for the food. They scramble for it. The pigeons flap their wings and push the smaller sparrows aside. The sparrows hop around the pigeons hoping they too will get to eat. The pigeons peck away at the grain with no concern for the sparrows. A peacock arrives and the pigeons also retreat. The food is gone. The peacock and even the pigeons fly off contentedly. The sparrows have gone hungry. Maybe tomorrow they may have a chance.

The second picture (Figure 10.2) is the story of the free market and the trickle-down effect. The process of 'cumulative causation' operates. When opportunities are opened up, those who have the wherewithal to take advantage of them—money, education, access to power—are the first to benefit. Their wealth and power increases faster than those left behind.

In this story, a woman scatters grain in her yard for the sparrows to eat. Some pigeons arrive and push aside the sparrows, then a peacock arrives and the pigeons move aside. All the birds look in awe at the peacock and admire its finery and its size and the sparrows hope that, after the peacock has eaten, there will be something left for them. The peacocks represent the wealthy, those whose expensive clothes and lifestyles are constantly being displayed in electronic and print media. Lists of the wealthiest people and the highest paid executives are widely published. They are admired, and described as leaders of the society and the economy.

SCENARIO III: TIGERS GROWLING

The third picture (Figure 10.3) is of a jungle. It is about the use and abuse of concentrated power, a condition which often arises as a reaction to the previous scenario (Figure 10.2). Frustrated by perceived injustices and the inability of democratic processes to address them, people will sometimes support dictatorial leaders who claim to take up their cause.

The tiger cannot be challenged by other animals and gets his way, while the wolves prey on the helpless smaller animals around him. As Lord Acton said, 'Power tends to corrupt, and absolute power corrupts absolutely.' Like wolves in the jungle, the families and friends of powerful leaders often feed on the little people who live in fear of them.

Figure 10.3: Tigers Growling (Scenario III)
The land has become a wild jungle. Bands of wolves roam. Small animals, and even big animals, live in fear of these marauding bands. Who can control them? Only the well-muscled and armed tiger is safe.

In this scenario, people who have the power to hurt others, and who are feared, are looked up to as leaders.

SCENARIO IV: FIREFLIES ARISING

The final scenario is fundamentally different. Unlike the others, it places the onus for driving change deeper in the system and does not rely on those at the top. India is a diverse, democratic

190 • *Redesigning the Aeroplane While Flying*

Figure 10.4: Fireflies Arising (Scenario IV)
At first, a few bright lights emerged from the darkness. Then many more. Soon the countryside is alight with dancing fireflies. It is wondrous to see how such tiny beings can transform the night. Where did they come from?

and complex system, and the theory of 'complex self-adaptive systems' suggests that such a dynamic entity cannot be controlled from a single centre. Change in India will be brought about by many hundreds of thousands of people taking the initiative at a local level, rather than waiting for an all-powerful (and, one hopes, benign) leader to emerge at the centre. The picture to represent this scenario is a hot, summer night in the Indian countryside

(Figure 10.4). Fireflies appear in the darkness and, as their numbers increase, the night is aglitter with myriad bright lights.

The fireflies represent Indians from all walks of life who take the first steps towards achieving change in their own lives and in the world around them, thereby inspiring others to do the same. Fireflies have already begun to arise in India. They are the leaders and they include the millions of women running self-help groups (SHGs), the growing number of social entrepreneurs, the small businesses, the socially responsible corporations and even the government officials who are bringing about change through innovation.

THE WAY FORWARD

All four paradigms of change co-exist in India. Buffaloes are wallowing; peacocks are strutting; tigers are growling; and fireflies are also arising. Which process of change, and what form of leadership, do we want more of?

Localization, Lateralization, Learning, and Listening, go with the model of leadership that is spread around in the 'Fireflies Arising' scenario (Figure 10.4). Systems must be reformed to support this model.

The India scenario of the 'Flotilla Advances', developed by the Planning Commission in 2012, is congruent with 'Fireflies Arising'. The National Council of Economic Research (NCAER) has computed that this scenario will give India the fastest, most inclusive and most sustainable growth.

India is at many confluences. Like other countries, it is at the confluence of the four forces that are creating a storm that is buffeting institutions of government and business not designed to withstand these conditions. It is at a confluence of civilizations of East and West. The fountainhead and home of many Eastern religions and philosophies, India was united into a modern nation with the English language, with which its intelligentsia has also connected very successfully with the Western world. India is at a noisy conflict of the ideologies of free markets and capitalism on one hand, and democracy and human rights on the other.

It is not the first time that India has encountered the contradictions between the principle of accumulation of wealth and power (the driving force of capitalism) and the principle of the rights of all living beings (democracy's core idea). Ashoka, the Mauryan emperor, had tried to reconcile the two, 2,300 years ago. He could not do so in his lifetime. Ashoka was one of history's earliest environmentalists too.

The goal of India's 12th Five Year Plan, that commenced in 2012, is 'faster, more inclusive and more sustainable growth'. India must reconcile all three requirements. It must find a solution to this 'tri-lemma' in its own way, as must all countries. What is India's vision?

A VISION OF INDIA

I very humbly offer a vision of India's future. It is a vision of an inclusive, democratic and capitalist India.

An Inclusive Democracy

In this vision, democracy will become deep and will become inclusive. Democratic governments are expected to be Governments Of the People, For the People, and By the People.

India has the largest electoral democracy in the world. India conducts elections on a scale that no other country comes close to. India's governments are elected by the people. Therefore, India has governments *of* the people in its states and at the national level.

People want their governments to be *for* the people too.

Indians are protesting that their governments are not accountable to the people. They are demanding transparency. They want to know what was done with the money that was supposed to be spent to improve public services and public infrastructure. This is the core demand of the anti-corruption movements. Therefore, governance reforms to make governments accountable to citizens have become imperative.

Deep democracy is government *by* the people—a democracy where citizenship is not merely the right to vote members of assemblies, but a democracy in which citizenship is also the active management by people of their own affairs in their communities and local bodies. Not an election time democracy, but a deliberative democracy in which citizenship is the right to understand the rules, and to shape the rules by which society governs itself.

Here India has a long way to go. When elected representatives say, 'You have elected us, now keep quiet and leave it to us till we come back for your votes next time,' they kill the very concept of deliberative, deep democracy.

Moreover, deep democracy requires elected and accountable governments in villages and in urban localities. The Indian Parliament passed the 73rd and 74th constitutional amendments twenty years ago. By these amendments, powers are required to be devolved to elected local bodies in villages and towns. But the country has not made much progress in implementing them.

An Inclusive Economy

India must become an inclusive economy. Genuine inclusion is not achieved by handouts and by redistribution. In fact, handing out and charity reinforce the idea of exclusion. Some are 'in' while others are 'out', and it is the moral responsibility of those who are 'in' to give to those who are 'out'.

Those who are excluded become genuinely included only when

they have equal opportunities to earn and live dignified lives and to contribute by their efforts too to the creation of wealth in society.

Just as institutions of government must be reformed to create an inclusive democracy, institutions of business and capitalism must be reformed to create an inclusive economy. Therefore, businesses must be not only *for* the people. They must also be *by* the people, and *of* the people.

To bring about inclusion, we need innovations that provide affordable and accessible goods and services, especially at the 'bottom of the economic pyramid'. This is the business opportunity for 'profit at the bottom of the pyramid' that C.K. Prahalad wrote about in *The Profit at the Bottom of the Pyramid* (2005), and that many entrepreneurs are pursuing. By producing products and services for poorer people, they can expand their customer base. For example, shampoo sold in a sachet, an innovation made by Hindustan Unilever, enabled even poor people to buy the company's products. The people pay. The profit from the bottom of the pyramid goes to the shareholders of the capitalist enterprise.

But this does not address the root cause of poverty. People are poor, and cannot afford to pay much, because they do not have incomes. They need jobs and incomes to lift themselves out of poverty. Therefore, they must be engaged in the processes of producing goods and services for themselves and others. And, therefore, we need innovations in production models that provide more jobs, so that business is *by* the people too.

Employees in enterprises owned by others have incomes, but do not share in the creation of wealth, the fruits of which go entirely to the owners. For a fuller inclusion in the benefits of growth, we need more enterprises in which the producers and workers share the wealth creation too. This requires innovations in enterprise design and governance models to shape businesses *of* the people. New forms of cooperatives and clusters are some emerging solutions.

In my vision, India, which is a country of over a billion democrats, will also be a country of hundreds of millions of capitalists.

Indeed this was Mahatma Gandhi's vision. His 'charkha' (spinning wheel) was a symbol. In his vision for India, all people would be producers of goods and services that the community and the market need. They would be earners and also owners of their enterprises, even if tiny.

Finally, in my vision, India will also be what Rabindranath Tagore envisioned in his memorable poem 'Gitanjali': a country not divided into fragments by narrow domestic walls. Indians are described as argumentative. *The Argumentative Indian* is the title of a book by the well-known Indian economist Amartya Sen. To create the India all Indians want, they will have to be less argumentative and more cooperative.

Indians must strive together towards 'the heaven of freedom' (another phrase from Tagore's 'Gitanjali')—a country in which every citizen has all three freedoms: political, social and economic freedom.

Everyone has work to do to reform the institutions they are in charge of, and in which they work. Some must lead and reform business corporations and other capitalist institutions. Others must lead and reform governments and government institutions. And many others must lead and reform institutions for democratic representation: political parties, civil society organizations and labour unions.

This vision sketches the institutional reforms we must make to reach our vision of a politically and economically inclusive nation. It is offered as a straw-man of a broad vision to induce a wider dialogue on a shared vision of India's future.

WHO WILL LEAD?

We need leaders who have the wisdom and the courage to reform the institutions they are given to lead. As Mahatma Gandhi said, we do not own institutions. We are their trustees. We must build society's trust in the institutions we lead.

I conclude with my definition of a leader. Leaders come in many shapes and they have many styles. Regardless of their shape, size and style, a real leader is she or he who takes the first steps towards what she or he deeply cares about, and in ways that others wish to follow.

Leaders are those who take the first steps. Not those who wait for others to lead. Great leaders have many followers because the steps they take are not towards selfish goals, but towards goals that others aspire to, too.

The heart of leadership is a deep caring for a cause. The awakening of leadership in each of us will arise when we look into ourselves and ask what we really care about deep down. Not what we are taught to care about by the manipulators of the carrots dangled before us and the wielders of the sticks to prod us—the 'incentives' that economists say make so-called 'rational' human beings do what they do. Carrots and sticks make us the tools of others. They are the means to make donkeys move, not humans.

The poet Robert Frost said, 'When to the heart of man was it less than a treason, to go with the drift of things, to yield with a grace to reason.'

We must look inside our hearts for what we want to make our world and our country for not only our own sakes, but for our children and grandchildren too. And we must stir our human aspirations to take steps now, together, to shape the future we want.

ACKNOWLEDGEMENTS

I want to thank many people who have helped me to shape the thoughts in this book. Most of all, I want to thank those who opened up new lines of inquiry into what makes great institutions. I have read innumerable books and papers for many years about the many facets of institutions and how they have been shaped; how great institutions have risen and how they have decayed. I would not have been able to learn so much if my deep interest in the nature of institutions had not been aroused early in my life. So it is those who opened my mind to where the seeds of great institutions lie that I want to acknowledge most of all.

I began my working life when I was twenty-two years old, as a young officer in Tata Administrative Services. The Tata Group was then, and remains, one of India's most respected institutions. Their organizational structures look much like the organizational structures of other companies. The buildings in which Tata companies house their factories and offices are very similar to those of others. The people who work in Tata companies are indistinguishable from people in other companies in how they look and the languages they speak. Though all the components with which Tata companies are constituted are the same as that of other companies, the Tata Group is considered a much greater Indian institution than any other Indian organization. Why? What is the secret ingredient?

I had the good fortune of working very closely with the vice chairman of the Tata Group, Sumant Moolgaokar, for twenty years.

He was acknowledged within the group as an institution builder par excellence. Over those years I also had several encounters with J.R.D. Tata, the chairman of the group, who shaped the Tata institution for over fifty years. Both these men left a great impression on me. What did these great institution builders focus on?

J.R.D. Tata walked the talk of values. The stories of the principled stands he took have shaped the culture of the group. He was a great person with humility who remained a learner all his life.

Way back in the 1970s, when India was yet 'an area of darkness', according to novelist V.S. Naipaul, Sumant Moolgaokar aspired to create an Indian automobile factory, designed and built by Indians, which would make all his countrymen proud. He realized his aspirations in the suburbs of Pune. When the plans for the Pune factory were being drawn up, Moolgaokar attended to every detail. He wanted excellence. Even Naipaul admitted that the Tata factory in Pune (which he visited) was a world apart from the rest of India.

When the factory blueprints were ready, Moolgaokar pointed out to the planners that they had missed the most essential ingredient of an institution: the people who would create it. Where would these people come from, he asked? What values would they learn to live by? How would they learn to respect the environment, and to care for the communities around the factory? What would motivate them to keep learning at work and to continuously improve their own capabilities? He entrusted me with the responsibility to shape the human side of the enterprise. And when I balked at being elevated to a position above many more experienced people, he advised me: 'Maira, you do not have to teach the people who work for you. Learn from them and they will respect you.'

Zen masters have a very effective, albeit unusual way of

teaching. They challenge their pupils to find an answer to a puzzle (a 'koan'). After months or even years of struggling with the koan, the students discover that the puzzle is not soluble. They also realize that the purpose of the exercise is the insights they obtain while trying to find the answer, not the solution. I thank Dr Manmohan Singh, the prime minister of India, for setting me on a Zen-like learning journey. Firstly, he took the risk of bringing me into the Planning Commission, even though I was not an economist, had never held any public position, and was not close to the ruling political formation. Then he gave me my koans. One was to find a way to reform the Planning Commission. It was urgently in need of reform, he said. But all efforts to do so had failed so far. The second koan was nested within the first. This was to discover how to make the Planning Commission useful to modern India by—in his words—converting it into a 'systems reforms commission' and 'an essay in persuasion'.

India is a large and very complex system. Systemic, institutional reforms are necessary for it to progress. India is also an energetic, insuppressible democracy. For India to progress as one nation, its discordant democrats must become able to persuade each other and align their forces towards common goals. What institutional reforms does India need? What processes for democratic deliberation must it use? Moreover, what can a Planning Commission do to make these happen? The koans he gave me went to the heart of the matter. They lit up my path to understanding what institutions are and how they can be changed.

There are many others who have been lampposts along my path of learning. It is not possible to name all. I mention only a few.

While people are the heart of any institution, they are given shape by the norms and the rules that govern the behaviour of their members. U. Sundarajan, chairman and managing director of Bharat Petroleum Corporation Limited, an Indian public sector company, who was my client, pushed me to discover the variety of rules and norms that can shape institutions. He was determined to make his company the fastest learning organization in the industry, so that it would get ahead of any new competitors that entered the Indian market which was being opened up to private sector and foreign companies in the 1990s. He had to live with unchangeable government rules. He could not alter the composition of his board and his executive team. Nor could he change the remuneration structure of the organization. Yet, he had to motivate his people. He stirred their deep aspirations to prove they could be the best, even though they were not the best paid. Along with his people, he shaped a new institutional culture of rapid learning and high performance in spite of the structural constraints they had to live with.

The Self-Employed Women's Association (SEWA) is globally admired for the spirit of sisterhood that has enabled it to empower millions of women economically and socially. Ilabehn Bhat, founder of SEWA, and her colleagues, Reema Nanavati and Renana Jhabwala, highlighted some essential qualities of SEWA for me. Its members, many of whom did not have a formal education, systematically learn to become leaders of large scale initiatives. They learn skills to develop consensus. And they learn how to organize to get things done. Together they shape a great institution.

I first met Arvind Kejriwal in January 2006 along with my colleagues in the International Futures Forum, who were on a learning journey in India to understand what new forces may change the country. He was then a leader of Parivartan, a local NGO, long before he rose to the national stage as a lieutenant of Anna Hazare in the anti-corruption movement in India and then as leader of the Aam Aadmi Party. We discussed how movements for changing institutions can be scaled up, or rather 'spread around' as Arvind suggested. I met Arvind again recently after he was suddenly made the chief minister of Delhi. He admitted that the structures for managing movements, political parties and governments are inherently different. The questions were: how does one build them and how does one change them?

I must acknowledge many organizations whose mission is to bring together like-minded people to explore how the world can be improved by reshaping institutions, who have been floodlights on my journey. These organizations include the International Futures Forum in Scotland, the Tallberg Forum in Sweden, the Bertelsmann Foundation and the Global Economic Symposium in Germany, the Aspen Institute in the US and the UN Global Compact.

I have not mentioned here the names of scores of other people who have contributed to shaping my ideas in this book, by their writings, the examples of their lives, and their guidance to me. I thank them all too.

I must thank the publishers of my previous books, in which I have developed my ideas on institutions, some passages from which I have incorporated into *Redesigning the Aeroplane While Flying*. These are McGraw Hill International (*The Accelerating Organization*), John Wiley and Sons (*Shaping the Future*), Penguin Books (*Discordant Democrats*) and Nimby (*Transforming Capitalism*).

Finally, I have to thank Ritu Vajpeyi-Mohan, the publisher of this book. Ritu has been keeping an eye on me the past five years. She said my vantage point in the Planning Commission would give me a perspective to put my ideas together and that she would have a book from me when I was ready. A year ago she told me the time had come to deliver!

Here is the book. I dedicate it to all my teachers. The credit for what is good in it goes to them. The flaws in it are my failings.

REFERENCES

Berlin, Isaiah (1996). 'On Political Judgement', *New York Review of Books*, 3 October.

Berners-Lee, Tim (2000). *Weaving the Web: The Original Design and Ultimate Destiny of the World Wide Web*, San Francisco: Harper Business.

Bruggman, Jeb (2009). *Welcome to the Urban Revolution*, Noida, India: HarperCollins.

Fishkin, James (2009). *When the People Speak: Deliberative Democracy and Public Consultation*, Oxford University Press.

Friedman, Thomas (1999). *The Lexus and the Olive Tree*, Picador.

———(2005). *The World is Flat*, London: Allen Lane.

Fromm, Erich (1978). *To Have Or To Be?* London: Jonathan Cape.

Fukuyama, Francis (1992). *The End of History and the Last Man*, Free Press.

———(2011).*The Origins of Political Order*, New York: Farrar, Strauss and Giroux.

Gandhi, Gopalkrishna and Rupert Snell (eds) (2007). *Gandhi is Gone, Who Will Guide Us Now?* Ranikhet, India: Permanent Black.

Gardner, Howard (1983). *Frames of Mind: The Theory of Multiple Intelligences*, Basic Books.

Goleman, Daniel (1996). *Working with Emotional Intelligence*, Bloomsburg Publishing.

Gray, John (1998). *False Dawn: The Delusions of Global Capitalism*, New York: The New Press

Greenspan, Alan (2013). 'Never Saw it Coming: Why the Financial

Crisis took Economists by Surprise', *Foreign Affairs*, November/December.

Hamilton, Alexander, James Madison and John Jay. *The Federalist Papers,* 85 articles published in *The Independent Journal* and *The New York Packet* between 1787-1788.

Hirschman, Albert O. (1970). *Exit, Voice, and Loyalty*, Cambridge, Massachusetts: Harvard University Press.

Hock, Dee (2005). *One From Many: VISA and the Rise of Chaordic Organization*, San Fransisco: Barret-Koehler Publishers.

Jacobs, Jane (1994). *Systems of Survival*, New York: Vintage Books.

Jordan, Luke, Sébastien Turban and Laurence Wilse-Samson (2013). 'Learning with the State: A Research Agenda', draft prepared for 'Making Growth Happen: Implementing Policies for Competitive Industries', 16–17 October 2013, World Bank, Washington, DC.

Layard, Richard (2005). *Happiness: Lessons from a New Science*, New York: Penguin.

Lijphart, Arend (1999). *Patterns of Democracy: Government Forms and Performance in Thirty-Six Countries*, London: Yale University Press.

Mahbubani, Kishore (2008). *The New Asian Hemisphere: The Irresistible Shift of Global Power to the East*, New York: Public Affairs.

Nace, Ted (2003). *Gangs of America: The Rise of Corporate Power and the Disabling of Democracy,* San Fransisco: Berrett-Koehler Publishers.

North, Douglass C. (2010).*Understanding the Process of Economic Change*, Princeton: Princeton University Press.

Prahalad, C.K. (2005). *The Profit at the Bottom of the Pyramid*, Singapore: Wharton School Publishing.

Sachs, Jeffrey (2011). *The Price of Civilization: Economics and Ethics after the Fall,* London: The Bodley Head.

Scott-Clark, Cathy and Adrian Levy (2013). *The Siege: 68 Hours Inside the Taj*, Penguin Books.

Scott, James (1998). *Seeing Like a State*, New Haven: Yale University Press.

Silver, Nate (2012). *The Signal and the Noise*, Penguin Press.

Stieglitz, Joseph E., Amartya Sen and Jean-Paul Fitoussi (2010). *Mismeasuring our Lives: Why GDP Doesn't Add up*, New York: The New Press.

Thurow, Lester (1997). *The Future of Capitalism: How Today's Economic Forces Shape Tomorrow's World*, London: Penguin Books.

The Economist (2001). *The Economist Technology Quarterly*, 24 March.

Turner, Adair (2012). '2010 Lionel Robbins Memorial Lectures' published in *Economics After the Crisis: Objectives and Means*, Cambridge, Massachusetts: MIT Press.

Vajpeyi, Ananya (2012). *Righteous Republic: The Political Foundations of Modern India*, Cambridge, Massachusetts: Harvard University Press.

Waldorp, Mitchel (1992). *Complexity: The Emerging Science at the Edge of Order and Chaos*, New York: Simon and Schuster.

Wilkinson, Richard and Kate Pickett (2009). *The Spirit Level*, New York: Allen Lane.

Wilson, E.O. (2013). *The Social Conquest of Earth*, W.W. Norton & Co.

Made in the USA
Monee, IL
03 May 2026

49438705R00135